Rescued by...

Upgrading Your PC

Kris Jamsa, Ph.D.

JAMSA P·R·E·S·S
...a computer user's best friend

a division of Kris Jamsa Software, Inc.

Published by
Jamsa Press
2821 High Sail Ct.
Las Vegas, NV 89117
U.S.A.

For information about the translation or distribution of any Jamsa Press book, please write to Jamsa Press at the address listed above.

Rescued by Upgrading Your PC

Printed in the United States of America.
987654

ISBN 1-884133-04-5

Publisher	*Technical Editor*
Debbie Jamsa	Kevin Hutchinson
Copy Editor	*Illustrator*
Paul Medoff	Jeff Wolfley & Associates
Composition	*Indexer*
Ken Cope	Konrad King
Cover Design	*Cover Photograph*
Swan + Logan Advertising	O'Gara/Bissell
Layout Design	*Technical Advisor*
Discovery Computing, Inc.	Phil Schmauder

Fulfillment and distribution of Jamsa Press books is managed by Discovery Computing Inc. For more information call 1-800-628-8280.

Table of Contents

GETTING STARTED WITH PC UPGRADES

Since you've picked this book up, it's reasonable to assume that you may be wondering if you can really upgrade your own PC. The lessons in this section not only show you that you can perform upgrades yourself, they also get you started. In fact, before you finish Lesson 1, you will have performed your first PC upgrade! By the time you finish Lesson 2, you will be able to open your system unit and identify the key components. So, put your fears aside and let's get started. As you will find, upgrading your PC is actually very easy. The lessons presented in this section include the following:

Lesson 1 *Getting Past Your Fears (You Can Do This)*

Lesson 2 *Opening Your PC's System Unit*

Lesson 3 *Understanding Your Computer's Ports*

Lesson 4 *Understanding the PC's Expansion Slots*

Lesson 5 *Working with Boards and Chips*

Lesson 6 *Understanding Your Computer's CMOS Memory*

Lesson 7 *Replacing Your PC's CMOS Battery*

Lesson 1

Getting Past Your Fears (You Can Do This)

If you own or work with a computer, the bad news is that your computer is already obsolete. Computer technology changes so fast that by the time you unpack a new computer, faster and more powerful systems are available. The good news, however, is that if your computer lets you perform your work, you can relax. The lessons presented throughout this book will show you several ways you can improve your existing computer's performance, without spending a dime! In addition, you will learn fast and inexpensive hardware upgrades you can perform yourself to improve your system's speed without spending a bundle.

There are several new capabilities sweeping computer communities that include multimedia, computer-based faxes, and online access to the information superhighway. To make the most of your computer, you will eventually need a CD-ROM drive, a sound card, a fax/modem, and more memory. By following the step-by-step instructions presented throughout this book, you can easily perform these key upgrades yourself, saving a bundle.

You don't have to be a computer genius to perform the upgrades discussed in this book. In fact, you don't even have to like your computer. By working a lesson at a time, you will find that performing most upgrades is easy. In fact, after you have one or two upgrades under your belt, you will find your PC much less frightening. Also, when you experience the increased productivity that follows an upgrade, you'll wonder how you ever got along without it.

This lesson helps you "break the ice," letting you understand that, regardless of your level of expertise, you can perform computer upgrades yourself. By the time you finish this lesson, you will understand the following key concepts:

- What it means to upgrade your PC
- Why you will need to upgrade your PC
- When upgrading is not cost effective
- Steps you need to take before you begin an upgrade
- How upgrading your PC affects your warranties and registrations
- Common tools of the trade
- Performing your first upgrade is as easy as plugging in a hair drier

The best way to get started is to begin. So, let's begin.

WHAT IT MEANS TO UPGRADE YOUR PC

Ask ten different users what it means to upgrade a PC, and you will probably get ten different answers. Everyone has a different view of upgrading a PC, based on their current needs. To the user who is getting started with multimedia, upgrading a PC might mean adding a CD-ROM drive and sound card. Likewise, to a traveling salesperson, upgrading a PC might mean adding a fax/modem. Finally, to a computer programmer, upgrading a PC might mean installing a new Pentium processor.

Upgrading your PC is simply the process of installing new hardware or software that improves your computer's ability to serve your needs. This book examines several different ways you can upgrade your PC. In some cases, the upgrade will require new hardware. In other cases, you might need to install new software. Finally, there will be some cases when you simply need to put your existing software to better use.

UPGRADING PC SOFTWARE

One of the most important PC upgrades you need to know how to perform is how to install or upgrade software. Just as many users don't feel comfortable with their PC's hardware, many feel even less comfortable with software—the programs your computer runs. As a result, many users still run old software because the current software "meets their needs" and because they have never performed a software upgrade.

In Lesson 30, you will learn how to perform software upgrades. As you will learn, installing software programs is actually very easy—software manufacturers work hard to make it easy. Like hardware upgrades, after you install one or more software programs, you will become very comfortable with the process. As a result, you will no longer be dependent on someone else upgrading your software for you!

IT'S HARD TO HURT YOUR PC

Many users hesitate to upgrade their PC because they are afraid of "breaking it." As it turns out, it is harder to damage your PC than you might guess. If you follow the steps presented in this book, you will not hurt your PC. So, treat you system with care, but don't be afraid to perform the operations discussed in the lessons of this book. In that same light, however, if something is not broken, don't fix it. Until you have more experience, don't experiment.

WHEN YOU SHOULD UPGRADE YOUR PC

PC upgrades help you maximize your existing computer's capabilities. In some cases, you will upgrade your PC to improve its performance. In other cases, your upgrade will add new capabilities such as a CD-ROM drive, sound card, or fax/modem.

Software upgrades occur for one of two reasons. First, some upgrades simply fix errors (called *bugs*) that were present in the previous versions. Normally, software manufacturers will offer such upgrades for free or for a very nominal price. Second, major software upgrades add new features to the software program. As a rule, you should normally upgrade your software to the latest version.

When you are adding a new hardware capability, you have already identified your need for an upgrade. When you are upgrading to improve your system performance, you must first identify your computer's *bottlenecks* (the devices that slow down your PC). Use the following symptom list to determine where you should focus your initial upgrade efforts:

1. Programs start slowly after you type the program name at the DOS prompt or when you double-click on a program icon within Windows—see Lesson 34 on defragmenting your disk.

2. You experience considerable delays when switching from one program to another from within Windows—see Lesson 35 on fine-tuning Windows.

3. You are constantly struggling due to insufficient disk space—see Lesson 32 on compressing your hard disk.

4. Your monitor's sharpness does not match that of another computer—see Lesson 19 on upgrading your monitor and Lesson 20 on upgrading your PC's video card.

5. You experience delays when a program reads or writes to a file—see Lesson 31 on installing disk-caching software.

6. Your system does not start—see Lesson 27 on troubleshooting your PC.

7. You run two or more programs within Windows on a regular basis—see Lesson 13 on adding memory to your system.

> ### UPGRADING DOES NOT MEAN REPAIR
>
> Sometimes you will have a choice as to when you perform your upgrades. At other times, you will turn on your computer and . . . nothing. When you computer fails to start or when a hardware device stops working, you'll need to determine the cause. In Lesson 27, you will learn how to troubleshoot the most common PC problems. After you identify the source of an error, you will need to determine how best to correct it.
>
> With hardware costs constantly decreasing, you will normally find it less expensive to replace, rather than repair, hardware. In fact, by following the lessons presented in this book, you can perform many such replacements yourself. Unless you happen to be a hardware technician, you won't be able to repair most PC hardware devices.

WHEN UPGRADING IS NOT COST EFFECTIVE

Just as computer capabilities constantly change, so too do computer prices. As such, there will be many times when you must weigh the cost differences between upgrading your existing hardware and simply purchasing a new system. For example, if you are adding multimedia capabilities, you might need to determine whether your current system can handle multimedia applications. As a general rule, if your computer is less than three years old and you simply want to improve your existing capabilities, you should upgrade. For example, if you use your computer to perform word processing, you can normally improve your system's performance by adding memory (see Lesson 13), adding disk-caching software (Lesson 31), or by defragmenting your disk (Lesson 34).

If you are adding new capabilities, however, you need to decide whether the upgrade is cost effective or whether you should purchase a newer system. As a general rule, if your upgrade exceeds $300, you should evaluate a new system purchase. For example, adding a $150 fax/modem to your computer can greatly increase your existing computer's capabilities. However, if you are considering a multimedia upgrade kit that includes a CD-ROM and a sound card, you might not be satisfied with your existing computer's performance.

How should you decide when to upgrade or replace your PC? In general, when you shop for new hardware, ask the salesperson how a computer's type (such as a 386 or 486) affects the device's performance. In the case of a fax/modem, for example, your computer type will have no impact. For a multimedia upgrade, however, the faster your PC, the greater its multimedia capabilities.

> ### BEFORE YOU REPLACE YOUR COMPUTER
>
> Before you decide to replace your computer, make sure that you have "fine-tuned" your PC's existing capabilities. Specifically, make sure that you have
>
> 1. Defragmented your hard disk (see Lesson 34)
> 2. Installed disk-caching software (see Lesson 31)
> 3. Fine-tuned Windows (see Lesson 35)
> 4. Maximized your computer's memory use (see Lesson 33)
> 5. Doubled your computer's current disk space (see Lesson 32)
> 6. Used the most recent version of your software programs (see Lesson 30)
>
> To maintain maximum PC performance, you might need to tweak several of these settings on a regular basis.

BEFORE YOU GET STARTED

After you perform one or two hardware upgrades, you will feel comfortable with the upgrade process. Thus, when you perform subsequent upgrades, you may be in a hurry to get started. Put your desire to get started aside and take time to create a good working environment. To begin, make sure you are working in a well-lit area. When you install different hardware boards, you might need to change small on-board switches. If you can't see the switches, you might end up spending a great deal of time trying to troubleshoot why the board does not work. In addition, you will want room to spread out your computer pieces. Likewise, make sure you have the proper tools of the trade, as discussed next.

TOOLS OF THE TRADE

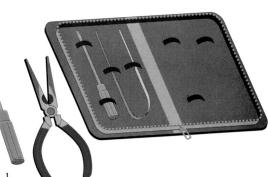

Before you perform any of the upgrades presented in this book, you should spend a few dollars to get the right set of tools. Almost any computer store will sell a computer tool kit for less than $20. Purchase such a kit and place it in the drawer next to your computer. Should you ever need to perform an upgrade, you will have all the tools you need.

In addition, locate several empty pill containers. When you later perform an upgrade, you can place the screws you remove into related pill containers. By taking time to organize screws in this way, you will save considerable time you might otherwise spend looking for lost screws.

PERFORMING YOUR FIRST UPGRADE

Your first hardware upgrade is one of the most important upgrades you will ever perform and also the easiest. If your computer is not currently plugged into a surge suppresser, put down this book and run to the computer store!

A surge suppresser protects your computer from electrical surges that travel down power lines, normally as the result of lightning. In short, the surge suppresser prevents the surge from reaching your computer.

Suppresser

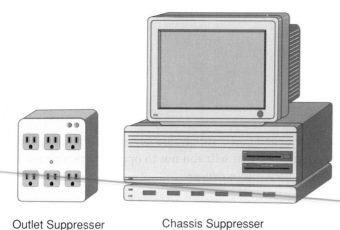

Although their sizes and shapes may differ, there are two primary surge suppresser types. The first surge suppresser plugs directly into the wall outlet. The second suppresser type typically sits beneath your monitor or PC.

The advantage of this second type is that it typically includes on/off switches for each plug, letting you control each hardware device.

Outlet Suppresser   Chassis Suppresser

To install a surge suppresser, perform these steps:

1. Exit all running programs and turn off your computer.

2. Unplug your computer and other devices, such as your monitor and printer.

3. Plug in your surge suppresser.

4. Plug your computer and other devices into the surge suppresser.

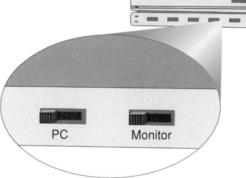

After you install your surge suppresser, you may be able to turn your computer on or off either using the computer's own on/off switch or the on/off switch found on the surge suppresser.

WHAT TO LOOK FOR WHEN BUYING A SURGE SUPPRESSER

As you shop, you may find several different surge suppressers whose prices vary considerably. Before you choose a suppresser, consider the following capabilities:

1. Is the surge suppresser Underwriters Laboratories (UL) approved?

2. Make sure the device is a surge suppresser and not simply a power strip that simply provides more power outlets but no surge protection.

3. Does the surge suppresser provide on/off switches that let you control each outlet? Do you need such support?

4. Does the surge suppresser support modem phone lines? Remember, phone lines, too, are susceptible to carrying electrical spikes.

Note: If you travel with a laptop computer, you should purchase a small surge suppresser that you can take with you. In this way, you protect your computer resources while on the road.

UNDERSTANDING WARRANTIES AND REGISTRATION

Many users hesitate to perform hardware upgrades because they are concerned about damaging their computer or violating their computer's warranty in some way. If you follow the steps presented in this book, you will not damage your computer's hardware. Likewise, computer upgrades are a common occurrence. PC manufacturers sell computers with the knowledge that users will need to install new hardware boards over the PC's lifetime. By installing standard PC components, such as those discussed in this book, you should not violate your PC's warranty.

Note, however, that some PC components, such as your monitor and power supply, are never meant to be opened. In such cases, the hardware device should contain a warning message that tells you not to open it. Opening such a device will very likely violate the device's warranty and might place you in danger.

When you purchase new hardware or software, the package will normally contain a registration card. Always take time to fill out and return such cards. Manufacturers use the card to make you aware of new products and upgrades. In addition, some manufacturers may require receipt of the card before they will provide you with technical support.

WHAT YOU NEED TO KNOW

Almost every PC can be upgraded in one way or another. As long as your computer meets your current needs, you don't have to become obsessed with upgrading. However, by improving your computer's performance, you will very likely improve your own productivity. In addition, the next generation of computer programs (multimedia and telecommunications) will require you to make hardware changes. In the past, users had to determine when they could afford to upgrade their computer. In the future, you will need to decide when you can no longer afford *not* to upgrade.

In Lesson 2, you are going to open up your PC and get to know several different pieces. Before you continue with Lesson 2, however, make sure that you understand the following key concepts:

✓ In the simplest sense, upgrading your PC is simply the process of using hardware and software to get the most from your existing PC.

✓ Users upgrade PCs to add new capabilities or to improve their system's performance. If you are adding new hardware capabilities, you have already identified your need to upgrade. If you are upgrading to improve system performance, first identify bottlenecks within your computer.

✓ With the cost of computer hardware constantly decreasing, there may be times when it is more cost effective to invest in a new system than to upgrade an older system. When you plan to invest more than $300 on a hardware upgrade, you need to consider buying a new PC.

✓ Before you perform a hardware upgrade, make sure that you have a well-lit work space, a tool kit, and containers to hold screws you might remove from your system.

✓ PC manufacturers expect you to add new hardware boards to your system. Thus, you will not violate your computer's warranty by adding a fax/modem or sound board to your PC.

✓ Having the correct tools can simplify most PC upgrade operations. Before you perform an upgrade, purchase a tool set from your computer retailer.

✓ If your computer is not currently plugged into a surge suppresser, make a suppresser your first computer upgrade.

Lesson 2

Opening Your PC's System Unit

Your PC's system unit houses your computer's disk drives, memory, central processing unit (CPU), motherboard, and other hardware boards, such as a modem or sound card. When you perform hardware upgrades, you will need to open up your system unit. For most users, opening the system unit for the first time can be quite intimidating. However, after you look around inside the system unit once or twice, you'll find the process quite straightforward.

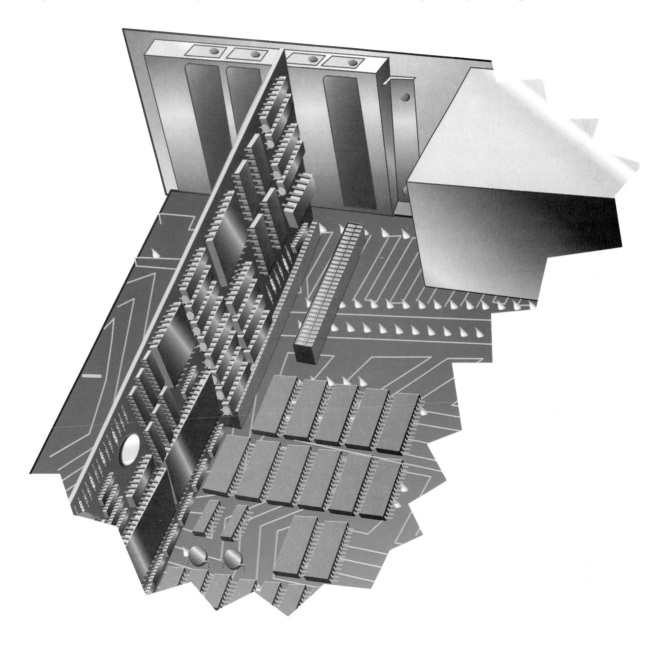

To help you become comfortable with opening your system unit, this lesson walks you through the steps you must perform. As you get started, relax. By following the steps presented within this lesson, you cannot hurt your system. By the time you finish this lesson, you will understand the following key concepts:

- Your system unit houses the PC's disk drives, central processing unit, memory, and other hardware devices

- Regardless of your PC type, the system unit contents are the same

- Before you open your system unit, you should turn off your PC and unplug your system

- To open your system unit, you simply need to remove the screws that hold on the unit's cover and then remove the cover

WHAT YOU'LL NEED

Before you get started with this lesson, make sure that you have the following readily available:

1. A PC tool kit with a screwdriver.

2. A container within which you can place the chassis screws.

3. A well-lit workspace with room for you to place the chassis.

Note: Never open up your system unit with the computer's power on. By working with the PC's power on, you not only risk damage to your system components, but also electric shock. In addition, you should unplug your system to further reduce your risks.

OPENING YOUR SYSTEM UNIT

If you examine the back of your PC, you should find several screws that hold on the system unit cover. Using a screwdriver, remove these screws, placing them into a container you can later quickly locate.

Note: To remove the system unit cover, you normally only remove the screws that are found on the outer edge of the system unit chassis.

Next, gently slide off the PC cover. The PC's system unit contains many cables. As you slide off the cover, make sure the cover does not hang up on one of the cables. In other words, if the cover does not easily come off, do not force it. After you remove the cover, place it to the side of your computer.

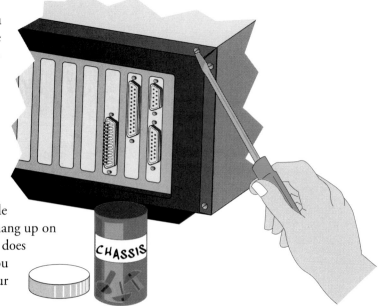

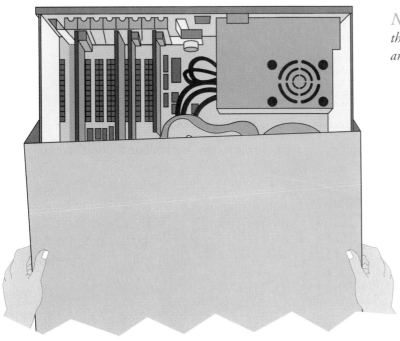

Note: As you slide the system unit cover off the PC, be very careful not to pull or stretch any of the PC cables.

WHAT YOU WILL SEE

Whether you are using a tower or desktop PC, the components you will find within a system unit are the same. Before you continue, take time to identify the key components discussed next.

Note: Before you touch anything, make sure that you touch the outside of your system unit chassis to ground yourself. In this way, you will greatly reduce the possibility of static electricity damaging one of your computer's internal cards or chips. You may want to purchase a clip that grounds your computer while you work. In this way, you reduce the chance of static "zapping" your chips! For information on purchasing such a ground, see your computer retailer.

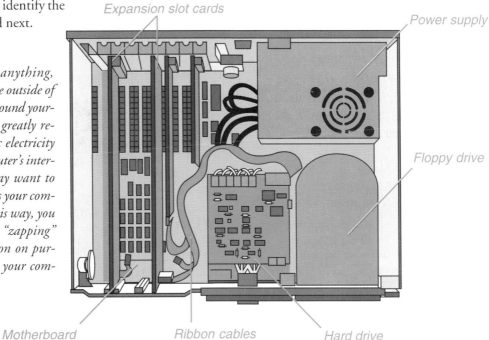

Expansion slot cards

Power supply

Floppy drive

Motherboard

Ribbon cables

Hard drive

RECOGNIZING THE MOTHERBOARD

Your computer's *motherboard* is the large flat electronic board that contains the majority of your computer's chips. In particular, the motherboard contains the CPU, the computer's electronic brain. The motherboard also contains the PC's memory. Before a computer program (software) can run, the program must reside within the computer's electronic memory. If you make extensive use of Windows, you can normally improve your system's performance by adding more memory. Lesson 13 examines PC memory in detail.

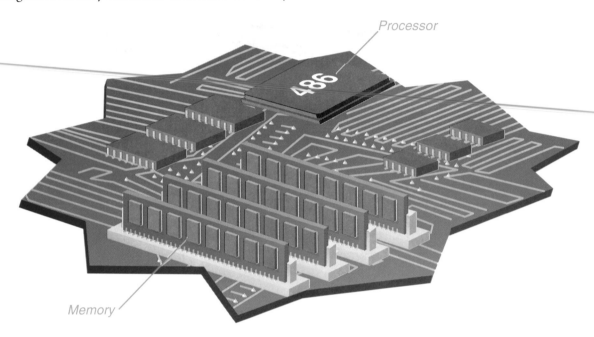

Processor

486

Memory

Of your computer's components, you need to treat the motherboard with the most care (it's normally the most expensive component). Although experienced users occasionally replace their computer's motherboard, such operations are best left to the experts and will not be covered within the lessons of this book.

RECOGNIZING THE POWER SUPPLY

Your computer is an electronic device where different parts work based on the presence or absence of electrical signals. When you plug your computer into your AC (alternating current that your house runs on), you actually plug in your computer's power supply. The power supply, in turn, turns the alternating current into the direct (one-way) current that your computer can use and disseminates this power to the rest of your computer. When electronic signals travel through your computer, the signals generate heat. As you can see, the power supply contains a fan that helps cool the PC.

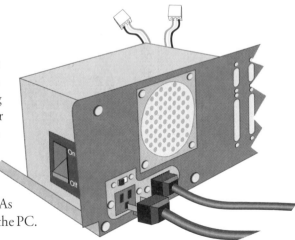

RECOGNIZING HARD AND FLOPPY DISKS

As you know, disks let your computer store information from one session to another. If you look closely, you will find that you can see a floppy disk within the floppy drive, but the hard disk is completely enclosed, hiding the media. Both disk drives are connected to the power supply. Likewise, most disks will have ribbon cables that connect the disk to the computer.

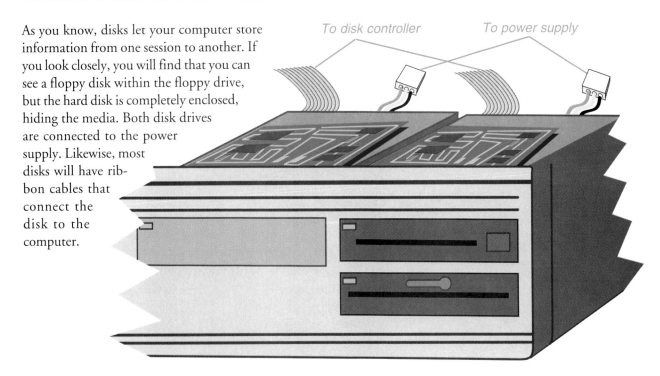

To disk controller   To power supply

RECOGNIZING THE EXPANSION SLOTS

Throughout this book, you will learn ways to add different hardware components, such as a modem or sound card to your PC. When you install a new hardware board, you will insert the board into one of the PC's expansion slots. Lesson 4 examines expansion slots in detail.

PUTTING YOUR SYSTEM BACK TOGETHER

After you have viewed your computer's inner components, you will need to replace your PC's cover. To do so, simply slide the cover back on to the PC. As before, take care not to damage any of the PC's ribbon cables. Next, replace the screws that secure the cover to the PC. Throughout this book, you will need to take your PC's cover off to install different hardware components. In such cases, simply follow the steps presented in this lesson.

WHAT YOU NEED TO KNOW

As you perform different upgrade operations, you will need to open your system unit. In this lesson, you may have opened your computer for the first time. With this experience under your belt, you are now well on your way.

In Lesson 3, you will learn more about your computer's ports which let you connect printers, mice, and other devices. Before you continue with Lesson 3, make sure you have learned the following key concepts:

✓ Your PC's system unit houses your computer's disk drives, memory, central processing unit (CPU), motherboard, and other hardware boards, such as a modem or sound card.

✓ Regardless of your hardware upgrades, you will need to open up your system unit. After you look around inside the system unit once or twice, you'll find that process quite straightforward.

✓ Whether you have a desktop or tower PC, the system unit contents are the same.

✓ Never open your system unit with your PC's power on or your PC plugged in.

✓ To open your system unit, you simply need to remove the screws that hold on the unit's cover. As you remove and when you later replace the system cover, take care not to damage cables within the system unit.

Lesson 3

Understanding Your Computer's Ports

When you connect other devices, such as a printer, to your computer, you connect a cable from the device to a *port* that appears on the back of your computer. Depending on the device, the type of cable you use to connect the device to your PC will differ. In this lesson, you will learn how to identify common port types quickly. By the time you complete this lesson, you will understand the following key concepts:

- How to locate your computer's ports
- The difference between male and female connectors and how to use a gender changer
- The purpose of common port types
- How to add ports to your computer

When you add hardware, you need to determine whether your computer will need additional ports. Thus, it is very important that you be able recognize common port types.

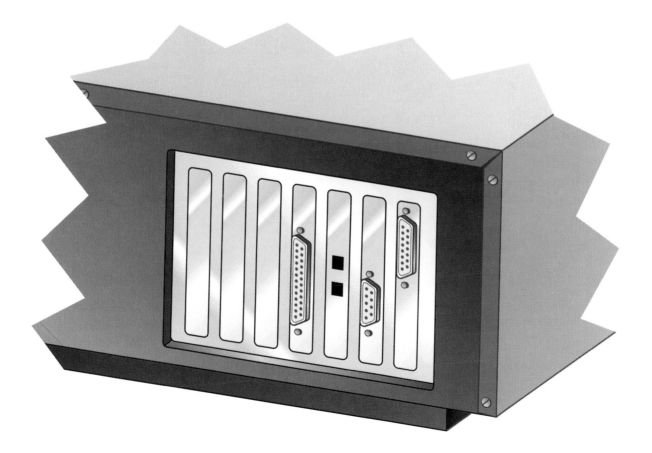

FINDING YOUR COMPUTER'S PORTS

A *port* is a connector that lets you connect a device to your PC. Ports let you connect devices such as a monitor, a mouse, a printer, or even a keyboard. If you examine the back of your PC, you will find several different ports. As you will learn, most PCs contain several common port types.

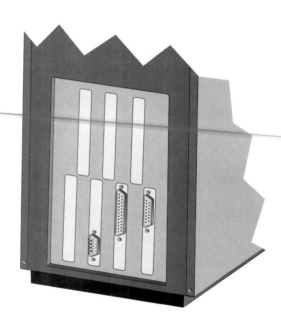

UNDERSTANDING MALE AND FEMALE PORTS

If you examine your PC's ports, you will note that some ports are designed to plug into a cable, while others are designed for a cable to be plugged into the port. Ports and cables, therefore, are classified as *male* or *female*, based on whether they plug in or are plugged into. A male cable or connector contains visible pins that plug in.

A female cable or connector, on the other hand, does not have such pins.

When you purchase a cable for a device, you need to examine your port type to ensure that you buy the correct cable (male or female). If you have a female port, buy a male cable. Likewise, for a male port, buy a female cable. To help you connect a cable to a port, ports and cables are shaped to ensure that you plug in the cable correctly.

Ports are often described by the number of pins they support. For example, common port types include 25-pin and 9-pin ports. When you shop for cables, or talk to a company's technical support staff, you might need to describe a port or cable. In such cases, you need to know the port's gender and the number of pins the port supports, such as a 25-pin male port.

USING A GENDER CHANGER

When you purchase a cable, you should purchase a male cable for a female port and a female cable for a male port. Should you purchase the wrong cable type, you can change a cable or port's gender using a *gender changer*. In other words, you can change a male cable into a female or vice versa with a gender changer.

Later in this lesson, you will learn how to recognize common PC port types. It is important that you understand the common port types. As you will learn, some port types look very similar, differing only by gender. If you use a gender changer with such a port, you can confuse the port's purpose.

RECOGNIZING COMMON PORT TYPES

PCs contain several common port types. This section examines several of these port types. Take time to compare the ports presented in this lesson to those found on the back of your PC. In fact, you might want to label your ports to help you later recall each port's purpose.

RECOGNIZING THE KEYBOARD PORT

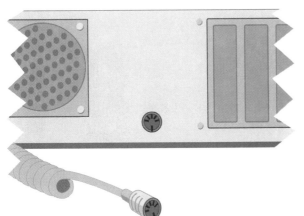

Like other hardware devices, you connect your keyboard to your computer through a port. Also, like most cables, you must align the keyboard cable pins with the port openings before you can connect the cable. Take time now to power off your computer (unpredictable results are possible if you leave the power on while plugging and unplugging the keyboard cable) and unplug your keyboard. Examine the cable and port. Align the cable's pins to the port and plug in the cable.

RECOGNIZING THE MONITOR PORT

Depending on your monitor type, your monitor will connect to either a 9- or 15-pin port. If you are using a older EGA monitor, your monitor will connect to a 9-pin port. If you are using a VGA monitor on the other hand, your monitor will connect to a 15-pin port.

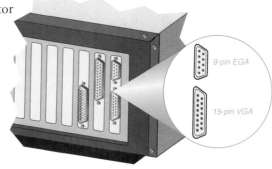

9-pin EGA

15-pin VGA

RECOGNIZING THE PRINTER PORT

You can connect a printer to either a parallel or serial port. *Parallel* ports are so named because they transmit data eight bits (binary digits) at a time, over eight wires. Because they transmit data eight bits at a time, parallel devices are much faster than their *serial* counterparts, which send all data through one wire in a *series*. PCs can support up to three parallel ports, named LPT1, LPT2, and LPT3. Parallel ports use a 25-pin female connector.

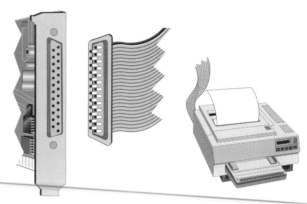

RECOGNIZING THE SERIAL PORT

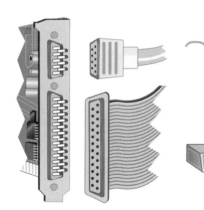

Serial ports can be used to connect devices such as printers, modems, a mouse, and more. As you just learned, however, because parallel ports are faster, most users connect their printers to parallel ports. Serial ports transmit and receive data one bit at a time. PCs can support up to four serial ports, named COM1, COM2, COM3, and COM4. However, most PCs only use two serial ports. Serial ports can be either 9- or 25-pin ports. In either case, the serial port uses a male connector.

If your PC only has a 25-pin serial port, but you have a 9-pin serial device, you can purchase an adapter that converts the 25-pin connector to a 9-pin connector and vice versa.

RECOGNIZING THE MOUSE PORT

As you will learn in Lesson 23, you can connect a mouse to a serial port, a bus mouse adapter, or a special proprietary port. Serial mice normally use a 9-pin serial female connector. A bus mouse and proprietary mouse both use small connectors that look like a small version of your keyboard cable.

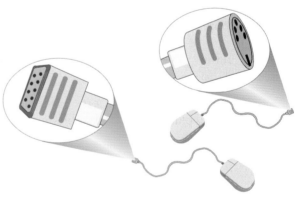

RECOGNIZING THE SCSI PORT

In Lesson 15 you will learn that a SCSI adapter provides you with a way to connect up to 7 high-speed devices such as a hard disk, CD-ROM, or tape drive. SCSI connectors normally use a 50-pin connector.

When you connect SCSI devices, you connect one device to the SCSI adapter and then connect other devices to each other, building a chain of devices.

HOW TO ADD PORTS TO YOUR COMPUTER

As you have learned, most PCs contain at least one serial port and one parallel port. Depending on the hardware you attach to your computer, there may be times when you need to add a new port. To add a port to your computer, you install a hardware board within your PC.

Before you install the second hardware board, you will need to change settings on the board that let the PC distinguish one similar board from another. Lesson 9 discusses the steps you must perform to change hardware settings.

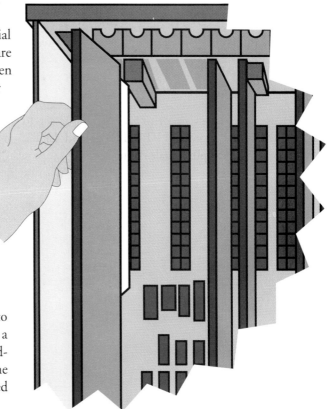

WHAT YOU NEED TO KNOW

When you connect other devices, such as a printer, to your computer, you connect a cable from the device to a port that appears on the back of your computer. Depending on the device, the type of cable you use to connect the device to your PC will differ. In this lesson, you learned how to identify common port types quickly.

In Lesson 4, you will examine your PC's expansion slots, which let you install hardware cards into your PC system unit. Before you continue with Lesson 4, make sure that you understand the following key concepts:

✓ If you examine the back of your computer, you will find the PC ports, which let you connect devices to the computer.

✓ Cables and port connectors are classified as male or female, based on whether the cable plugs in or is plugged into. Male cables and connectors have pins that plug into a female receptacle.

✓ When you describe a port connector or cable, you specify the gender (male or female) and the number of pins.

✓ If you inadvertently purchase the wrong cable type, you can use a gender changer to change a male connector to a female and vice versa.

✓ Regardless of your PC type, you will normally find at least one parallel and one serial port. Parallel ports are 25-pin female connectors. Serial ports are male connectors and can be 9- or 25-pin ports.

Lesson 4

Understanding the PC's Expansion Slots

When you install a card, such as an internal modem into your PC, you insert the card into an *expansion slot*, which consists of a *slot opening* in the chassis of the system unit and a *slot socket* on the motherboard. At first glance, you might think that one slot is the same as another. However, as you will learn in this lesson, that is not always the case.

This lesson examines the different expansion slot types. By the time you finish this lesson, you will understand the following concepts:

- How expansion slot types differ

- The purpose of a local bus

- The difference between an ISA, EISA, VESA, and PCI bus

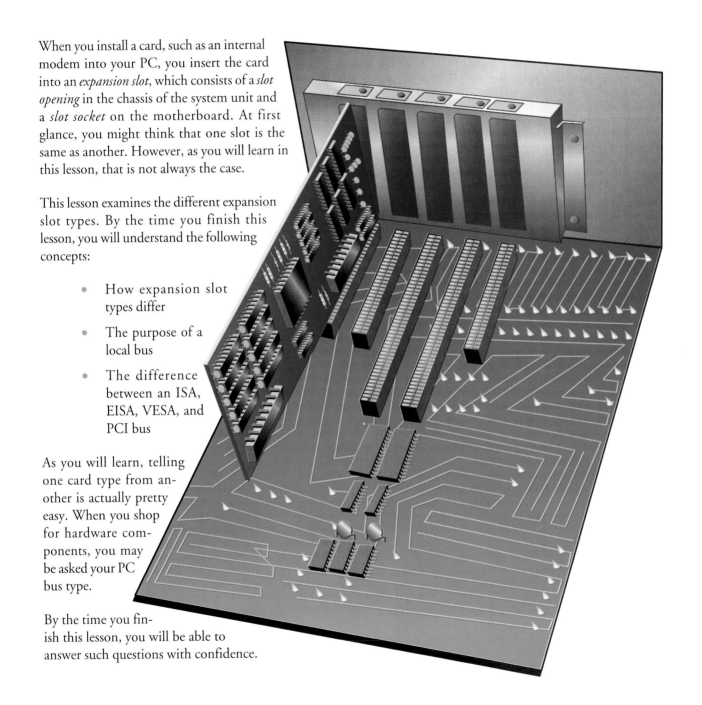

As you will learn, telling one card type from another is actually pretty easy. When you shop for hardware components, you may be asked your PC bus type.

By the time you finish this lesson, you will be able to answer such questions with confidence.

VIEWING YOUR SYSTEM'S EXPANSION SLOTS

Expansion slots reside within your PC system unit. To view your expansion slots, power off and unplug your PC. Remove your system unit cover as discussed in Lesson 2. Several of your PC's expansion slots may be in use, while others are available for use, as shown here:

If you examine the expansion slot openings, you will find that each has a small metal cover that is held in place by a small screw. This slot cover helps reduce the amount of dust that enters your system unit when the slot is not in use. When you install a card into an expansion slot, you first remove this cover. Hold onto the screw that held the cover in place. You will later use this screw to hold the card in the slot. Also, place the slot cover in a safe location. Should you ever remove the card, you will want to replace the cover.

When you insert a card into an expansion slot, never force the card into the socket. Instead, gently rock the card until it slides into place. After the card is in the slot, secure the card by replacing the screw that previously held the cover in place.

Available slots

RECOGNIZING BUS TYPES

When the IBM PC was first released in 1981, the PC communicated with expansion slot cards using eight bits of data at a time. The original *bus* (collection of wires) was called the ISA bus. ISA is an acronym for Industry Standard Architecture. In short, the ISA bus defines a set of rules (standards) the bus follows, as do card makers who design cards for the bus. In this way, when you buy a third-party card, such as an internal modem, the card will work within your PC.

When IBM released the 286-based PC AT, in 1984, the AT supported a 16-bit bus, also called an ISA bus. By supporting 16 bits of data at a time, this larger bus improved the PC's performance. Unfortunately, with the advent of faster 386 and 486-based PCs, the 16-bit bus became a performance bottleneck. As a result, many PCs started providing 32-bit EISA buses. EISA is simply an acronym for Extended Industry Standard Architecture. Because the 32-bit bus doubles the amount of data the bus can send, the EISA bus greatly improves system performance.

Unfortunately, as video cards increased their resolution and began to support a larger number of colors (up to 16 million), the PC bus still could not keep up. As a result, a new "local bus," which lets devices (such as a video card) talk directly to the CPU was designed. Initially, the local bus design and standards were controlled by VESA, the Video Electronics Standards Association. Cards that support the VESA local bus are called VL-Bus cards. Recently, however, a more powerful local bus design has been released by Intel. This newer bus, called the PCI local bus (for Peripheral Component Interconnect) may emerge as the future standard bus.

THE PC BUS SCORECARD

Keeping track of the different PC bus types can be a difficult process, which might require a scorecard. The following definitions might help you keep track.

Acronym	Name	Meaning
ISA	Industry Standard Architecture	16-bit expansion slot bus
EISA	Extended Industry Standard Architecture	32-bit expansion slot bus
VESA	Video Electronics Standards Association	Local bus that communicates directly with the CPU—sometimes called a VL-Bus
PCI	Peripheral Component Interconnect	Advanced local bus designed by Intel

---

DETERMINING A CARD'S TYPE

To determine a card's type by inspection, you need to examine the card's connectors. To begin, simple devices such as an internal modem or mouse use an 8-bit card. Many older PCs support 8-bit expansion slots. Newer PCs, however, use 16-bit and 32-bit slots instead.

A 16-bit ISA card adds a notch to the 8-bit card just shown and increases the number of pins on the card. In short, the 16-bit slot adds a second socket into which the card is placed.

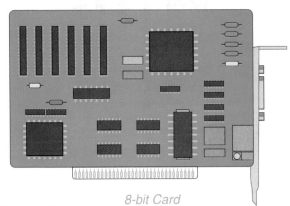
8-bit Card

A 32-bit EISA card is very similar in size and shape to the 16-bit card. However, if you examine the card closely, you will find that the card doubles the number of pins.

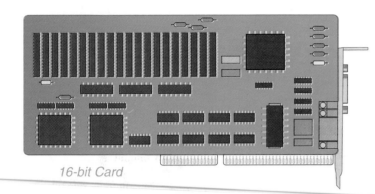

16-bit Card

As a general rule, you can place an 8-bit card into any expansion slot (8-bit, ISA, or EISA). Likewise, a 16-bit card can be placed into an ISA or EISA slot. A 32-bit EISA card, on the other hand, can only be used in an EISA slot.

A local bus card contains pins that slide into an expansion slot socket and pins that slide into the local bus. The most common local bus cards are high-speed video cards, discussed in Lesson 20.

As you shop for hardware boards, you need to be aware of your PC bus types.

WHAT ABOUT THE MICROCHANNEL?

If you use an IBM PS/2 computer, you will be concerned with another bus type called the Microchannel. In short, the Microchannel is a proprietary IBM bus. You cannot plug boards designed for the other buses discussed in this lesson into the Microchannel. Likewise,

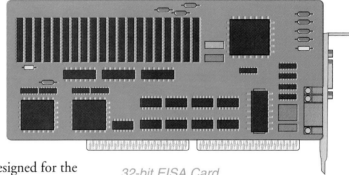

32-bit EISA Card

you can't use Microchannel cards in a standard PC bus. The disadvantage of the Microchannel is that it and its cards are not compatible with standard PC devices. The Microchannel's advantage is that it eliminates the IRQ conflicts that challenge PC users, as discussed in Lesson 8.

WHAT YOU NEED TO KNOW

In this lesson you learned about expansion slots, into which you plug various hardware boards, or cards, such as an internal modem or mouse card. Throughout this book, you will perform different hardware upgrades by working with cards and chips. In Lesson 5 you will examine the steps you should perform to work with chips and boards. Before you continue with Lesson 5, make sure you have learned the following key concepts:

✓ When you add a hardware card, you install the card into one of the PC's expansion slots, which each consist of a slot opening and a slot socket.

✓ PC expansion slots are not created equal. As the PC has evolved, so too has the bus (collection of wires) used to connect expansion slot devices to the PC.

✓ PC buses are classified as ISA, EISA, VESA, PCI and even the Microchannel. When you purchase a hardware card, you need to know your PC bus type.

✓ To improve video performance, many newer PCs support a local bus, which the CPU uses to directly access the video card memory, bypassing the expansion slots.

Lesson 5

Working with Boards and Chips

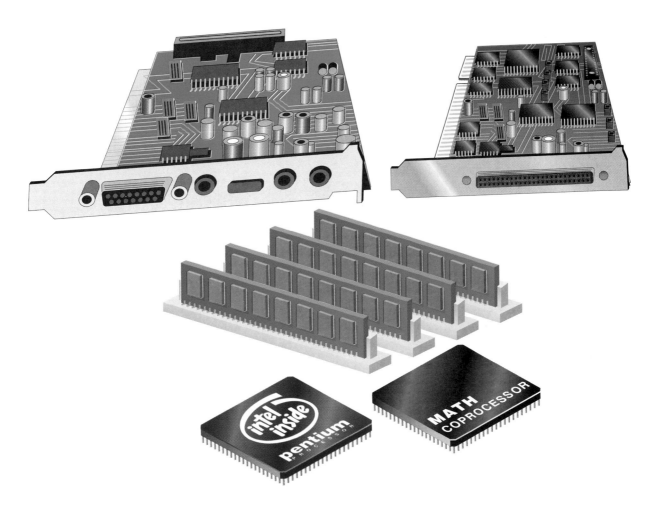

Throughout this book you will install different hardware boards and chips. If you have never installed a board or chip before, relax. Installing boards and chips is actually very easy. However, you do need to work with care. Electronics are fragile. As long as you don't apply "brute force" however, you should not have any problems. This lesson examines the steps you should perform to work with boards and chips. By the time you finish this lesson, you will understand the following key concepts:

- The need to have a chip extractor in your PC tool kit
- How to install a hardware board in an expansion slot
- How to remove a hardware board from an expansion slot
- How to install and remove chips
- How to create your own board and chip extractors

WORKING WITH HARDWARE BOARDS

When you perform hardware upgrades, such as installing an internal modem, sound card, or even a new video card, you will need to work with electronic boards, often called *cards*. A card has a tab with electrical connectors on it that slides into a socket on the motherboard. If the card is meant to be plugged into by a peripheral device, a port or ports will protrude from the slot opening in the chassis. In Lesson 3, you examined the PC's expansion slots, into which you install cards.

No matter which type of board you are installing, the steps you must perform are the same. To begin, turn off and unplug your PC. Next, remove your system unit cover, as discussed in Lesson 2. After you choose the slot into which you will insert the card, remove the small metal slot cover by unscrewing the screw that holds the cover in place. Store the screw in a safe place because you will later use it to secure the card in place.

Place the slot cover in a safe location. Should you later remove the card, you will want to replace the slot cover to reduce the amount of dust that enters the system unit.

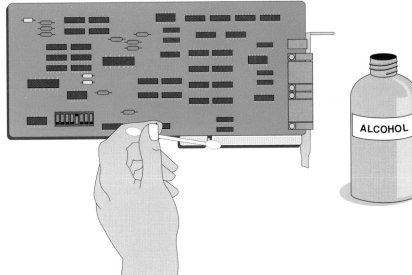

Examine the card you are going to install to ensure that the card's connectors are clean. Dirty connectors can prevent the board from working. To clean the connectors, use a Q-tip and rubbing alcohol.

Gently rock board into place

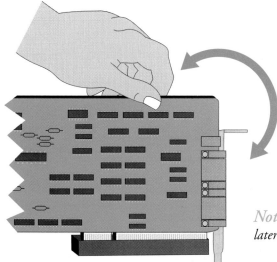

To install the card, gently slide the card's connectors into the expansion slot. You might need to rock the card slightly before the connector slides into place.

After the card is in place, secure the card by replacing the screw you previously removed. Next, replace and secure the system unit cover.

Note: If your board is shipped in a static-proof bag, save the bag so you can later use it should you ever remove the board from your PC.

INSTALLING A HARDWARE BOARD

Regardless of the type of board you are installing, the steps you must perform are the same:

1. Turn off and unplug your system unit.

2. Remove your system unit cover.

3. Select the desired expansion slot.

4. Remove and store the small metal slot cover, placing the screw in a safe location. Save the small metal slot cover in case you later need to replace it.

5. Gently insert the card's connector into the slot socket, securing the card in place with the screw that held the slot cover.

6. Replace and secure the system unit cover.

REMOVING A HARDWARE BOARD

The steps for removing a hardware card are almost identical to those just discussed, with a few exceptions. First, after you remove the card, protect the card by placing it back into its static-proof bag. Next, store the card in a safe location, ideally protected by a cardboard box.

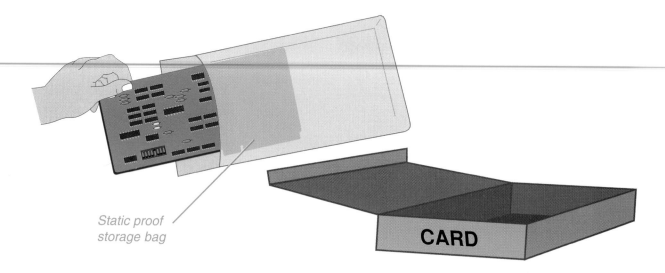

Static proof
storage bag

CARD

In some cases, you might have trouble removing a card from the expansion slot socket (don't forget to remove the slot cover screw, which now holds the board tight in the slot opening). If you have trouble, you might be able to remove the board from the slot gently using a bent flathead screwdriver as a sort of hook to gently pull each end of the board.

REMOVING A HARDWARE BOARD

No matter which type of board you are removing, the steps you must perform are the same:

1. Turn off and unplug your system unit.
2. Remove your system unit cover.
3. Remove the slot cover screw, which now holds the board tight in the slot opening.
4. Gently remove card from the expansion slot.
5. Place the card into a static-proof bag and then into a cardboard box.
6. Replace the expansion slot cover to prevent dust from entering the system unit.
7. Replace and secure the system unit cover.

WORKING WITH CHIPS

Depending on the upgrade you are performing, you may need to install or remove one or more chips. Before you begin, make sure that you are working in a static-free environment. Next, ground yourself by touching the system unit chassis.

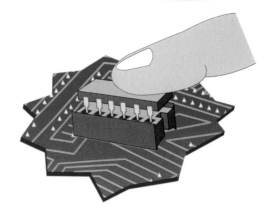

To insert a chip, you simply align the chip's pins with the corresponding sockets and gently slide the pins into place.

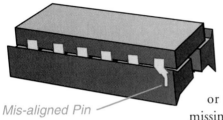

Mis-aligned Pin

As you insert the chip, make sure each pin is inserted successfully. If you are not careful, one or more pins will bend, missing the socket, or worse yet, breaking. If a pin is out of place, the chip will not work.

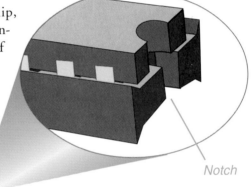

Notch

When you install a hardware board, correctly aligning the board is very easy. When you install chips, however, the correct alignment is not always obvious. If you examine a chip and its socket closely, you will normally notice small numbers.

To align the chip, align pin 1 with socket 1 and so on. If the chip is not numbered, many chips place a small notch next to pin 1.

The easiest way to remove a chip from a socket is to use a chip extractor, which lets you gently pull the plug from the socket.

If you don't have a chip extractor, you may be able to create a similar device by bending a small flathead screwdriver. Using the screwdriver, you can gently remove the chip, one end at a time.

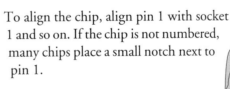

When you remove a chip, you might want to store the chip by gently pressing the chip's pins into a small piece of styrofoam. In this way, you reduce the chance of any pins getting bent.

WHAT YOU NEED TO KNOW

In this lesson you have learned how to install an expansion card into an expansion slot in your computer and a chip into its socket. You also learned how to remove them. In addition, you learned that a static electricity charge can destroy a chip or circuit board—make certain you discharge any static you have accumulated before you touch any components and work in a static-free environment.

In Lesson 6 you will examine your PC's CMOS memory contents. Your PC uses a special memory called the CMOS memory within which it stores key system settings, such as the number and type of your disk drives, the amount of memory, your video type, and even the current system date and time. The CMOS memory is battery powered, which lets your PC remember these settings even when it is powered off. Before you continue with Lesson 6, however, make sure you have learned the following key concepts:

- ✓ If you are shopping for a PC tool kit, look for one that includes a chip extractor.

- ✓ When you perform various hardware upgrades discussed throughout this book, you will need to remove and install hardware cards.

- ✓ When you install or remove a hardware card to or from an expansion slot, you may need to gently rock the board.

- ✓ When you install a chip, make sure that you do not inadvertently bend one of the chip's pins.

- ✓ If you do not have a chip extractor, you may be able to create a make-shift extractor by bending a small flat head screw driver.

- ✓ Static electricity can quickly destroy a chip or card. Never work with cards or chips without first grounding yourself by touching the system unit chassis. Also, you might want to consider buying and using a static mat.

Lesson 6

Understanding Your Computer's CMOS Memory

If you examine 100 different PCs, you might find as many different hardware configurations. Computers may differ by the number or type of floppy disks they contain, the type of video display, the amount of memory, and even their hard disk size. To help each computer keep track of its configuration, PCs use a special battery-powered memory called the *CMOS memory*. This lesson examines the CMOS memory contents and how you can update the memory settings. By the time you finish this lesson, you will understand the following concepts:

- Why the CMOS memory is battery powered

- How you can display your PC's CMOS memory contents

- How and when to update the CMOS memory settings

It is important that you understand the CMOS memory. When you add a disk or increase your computer's RAM, you will need to update your computer's CMOS settings. Until you update the CMOS, your PC will not be aware of hardware updates.

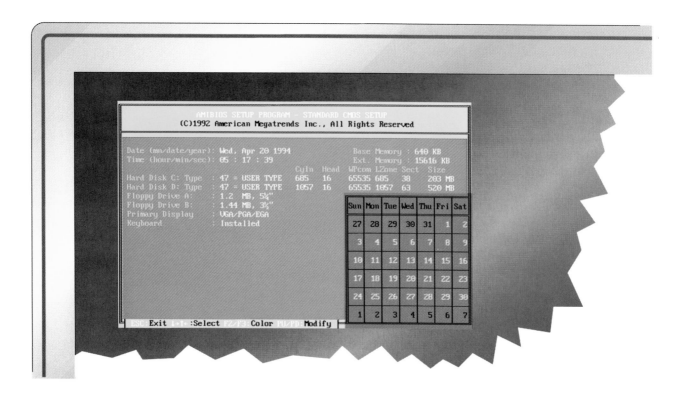

UNDERSTANDING THE CMOS MEMORY

CMOS is simply an acronym for complementary metal oxide semiconductor. CMOS simply describes the type of material from which this special memory is made. To start successfully, your PC needs to know specifics about its disk types, available memory, video type, and so on.

As you have learned, the information the PC's random access memory contains is lost when the PC's power is turned off. For the PC to remember its key settings, the PC uses a small battery-powered CMOS memory. Because the PC's CMOS memory is battery powered, the memory maintains its contents, even when the PC is unplugged.

HOW YOUR PC REMEMBERS KEY SYSTEM SETTINGS

PCs differ by the number and type of disks they contain, the amount of available memory, and more. When your PC starts, it needs to know these key settings. To remember these settings, the PC uses a small battery-powered memory called the CMOS. As you perform different hardware upgrades, you might need to update your system's CMOS settings.

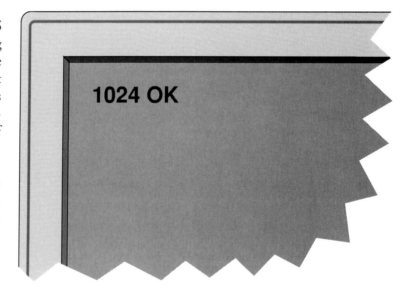

Your PC normally only uses its CMOS memory settings when it starts. Depending on your PC type, the way you access the CMOS settings will vary. When you first turn on your PC's power, the PC performs a self-test of its hardware components. During the self-test, the PC displays a count of its working memory.

Normally, you will access your system's CMOS settings by pressing one of the following keyboard combinations when your system completes its memory count:

- DEL
- ESC
- CTRL-ALT-ENTER
- CTRL-ALT-INS
- CTRL-ALT-ESC

Note: Some older PCs do not have a built-in setup program. Instead, you must boot (start) your computer using a special setup diskette to access the CMOS setup.

Depending on your system, your screen might display a menu of options, or it might immediately display the CMOS settings. If a menu appears, select the setup option. Next, your system will display a screen similar to that shown in Figure 6.1, which displays your current CMOS settings.

```
                  AMIBIOS SETUP PROGRAM - STANDARD CMOS SETUP
                  (C)1992 American Megatrends Inc., All Rights Reserved

     Date (mm/date/year): Wed, Apr 20 1994          Base Memory :  640 KB
     Time (hour/min/sec): 05 : 17 : 39              Ext. Memory :  15616 KB
                                          Cyln  Head  WPcom LZone Sect   Size
     Hard Disk C: Type   : 47 = USER TYPE  685    16  65535 685    38   203 MB
     Hard Disk D: Type   : 47 = USER TYPE 1057    16  65535 1057   63   520 MB
     Floppy Drive A:      : 1.2  MB, 5¼"
     Floppy Drive B:      : 1.44 MB, 3½"        Sun Mon Tue Wed Thu Fri Sat
     Primary Display      : UGA/PGA/EGA
     Keyboard             : Installed           27  28  29  30  31   1   2

                                                 3   4   5   6   7   8   9

                                                10  11  12  13  14  15  16

                                                17  18  19  20  21  22  23

                                                24  25  26  27  28  29  30

                                                 1   2   3   4   5   6   7

     ESC:Exit ↓→↑←:Select F2/F3:Color PU/PD:Modify
```

Figure 6.1 *System CMOS settings.*

As you can see, CMOS settings range from disk types to available memory. Also, the CMOS contains the current date and time. That's how the PC knows the current date and time, even after you turn off its power. Depending on your system, the steps you must perform to change a CMOS setting will differ. Read the instructions that appear on your screen display. In most cases, once you select a CMOS entry, you can change the entry's value using your keyboard PgUp and PgDn keys. After you change the entries you require, you can exit the setup program saving the new settings within the CMOS memory.

RECORD YOUR SYSTEM'S CURRENT SETTINGS

Eventually, the CMOS battery will fail. After you replace the battery, you must restore the CMOS settings. To simplify this task, you should write down your current system settings, placing the settings in a safe location. Should you later need to restore your CMOS settings, you will be very glad you took time to record the original values.

Note: If you have trouble invoking or using your PC's built-in setup program, you can purchase third-party software that lets you access the CMOS settings.

WHEN YOU NEED TO ACCESS CMOS ENTRIES

As long as your PC starts successfully, you can normally ignore the PC's CMOS settings. However, if you add memory to your system or install a new or different disk drive, you will need to update a CMOS setting. As you examine the lessons presented in this book, you will be instructed as to when you need to update the CMOS settings.

Your CMOS Battery Can Fail

Like all batteries, your CMOS battery will eventually die. When a CMOS battery fails, your system will display an error message similar to the following when you first turn on the PC's power:

```
Invalid System Settings—Run Setup
```

Should an error message similar to this appear, you will need to replace the CMOS battery by following the steps discussed in Lesson 7. After you replace the CMOS battery, you will need to restore the previous CMOS settings. At this time, you will be glad you recorded the CMOS settings as previously discussed.

Changing the CMOS Settings

When you install different hardware devices, you will need to update your PC's CMOS memory settings to inform the PC of the new hardware. Depending on your system, the steps you must perform to access the CMOS settings will differ. In most cases, you will press a specific keyboard combination immediately after your PC displays its available memory count when you first power on your PC.

Like all batteries, the PC's CMOS battery will eventually fail. In such cases, follow the steps discussed in Lesson 7 to replace the battery. Next, you must restore the CMOS settings by following the steps discussed in this lesson.

What You Need to Know

In this lesson, you learned about your computer's CMOS memory—what it is, what it is made of, how to change its settings, and when you need to.

Eventually, your PC's CMOS battery will fail. At that time, you will need to replace the battery. Lesson 7 examines the steps you must perform to replace your PC's CMOS battery. Before you continue with Lesson 7, make sure you understand the following key concepts:

- ✓ CMOS is an acronym for complementary metal oxide semiconductor. In short, CMOS defines the type of material from which the chip is made.

- ✓ Your PC uses a special memory called the CMOS memory to store specifics about your system, such as the number and type of disks, the amount of memory, the video type, and the current system date and time. If you change your hardware configuration, you might need to run the CMOS setup program to inform your computer of the changes.

- ✓ To access your PC's CMOS settings, you normally press a keyboard combination after your computer completes its power-on self-test.

- ✓ When you display your CMOS settings, write down the current values. Place your notes in a safe place. Should you ever need to restore the settings, you will be glad you took notes.

- ✓ Like all batteries, your CMOS battery will eventually fail. At that time, you will need to replace the battery and then restore the previous settings.

Lesson 7

Replacing Your PC's CMOS Battery

In Lesson 6, you learned that your PC uses a small battery-powered memory, called the CMOS, to remember different system settings when the PC's power is off. Like all batteries, the PC's CMOS battery will eventually fail, and you will need to replace it—fortunately, most CMOS batteries last several years. In this lesson, you will learn how to replace a CMOS battery. By the time you finish this lesson, you will understand the following key concepts:

- How to recognize a dead CMOS battery

- How to replace a CMOS battery

- How to restore your computer's previous CMOS settings

If you have not already read Lesson 6, which discusses the CMOS memory contents and how you access this special memory, do so now.

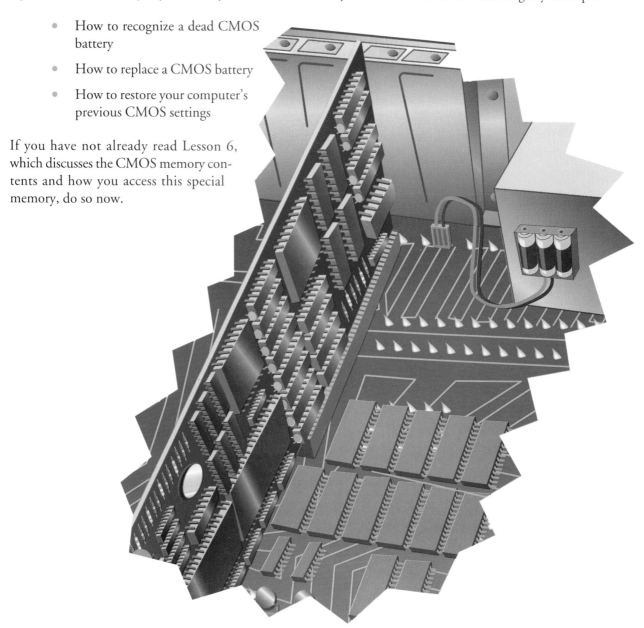

RECOGNIZING A DEAD CMOS BATTERY

The PC's CMOS memory stores such information as the hard disk type, the number and size of floppy disk drives, the amount of random access memory (RAM), and the current system date and time. When the CMOS battery fails, your PC will forget these key settings. When you next turn on your PC's power, your system will display an error message similar to the following:

```
Invalid System Settings—Run Setup
```

When this error message occurs, you need to replace the CMOS battery.

REPLACING THE CMOS BATTERY

PCs use one of two types of CMOS batteries. The first CMOS battery type is a small, flat, nickel-shaped battery. The second battery type looks more like a battery pack.

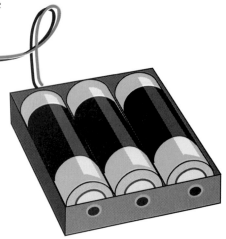

The CMOS battery resides within the PC's system unit. Follow these steps, discussed in Lesson 2, to open your system unit:

1. Turn off and unplug your PC.

2. Remove the screws that hold on the system unit cover, placing the screws in a safe location.

3. Gently remove the system unit cover.

Depending on your PC manufacturer, the location of the CMOS battery will differ. After you locate your CMOS battery, remove the battery and take it with you to your PC retailer. Purchase a similar battery type. If your system uses a battery-pack like CMOS battery, note the orientation of the wires that connect the battery to your PC's motherboard.

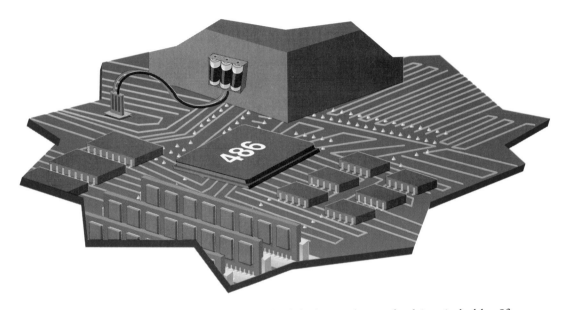

To replace the small nickel-shaped CMOS battery, simply slide the new battery back into its holder. If you are replacing a battery-pack like CMOS battery, make sure that you connect the battery cables to the motherboard in their original orientation.

RESTORING YOUR CMOS SETTINGS

When the CMOS battery dies, the PC forgets its key settings. After you replace the CMOS battery, you must restore the previous CMOS settings. To assign the CMOS settings, follow the steps discussed in Lesson 6.

REPLACING YOUR PC's CMOS BATTERY

Over time, your PC's CMOS battery will eventually fail. At that time, follow these steps to replace the battery:

1. Turn off and unplug the PC system unit.
2. Remove the system unit cover.
3. Locate the CMOS battery, noting the battery's cabling, if applicable.
4. Replace the battery, and if necessary, connect the new battery's cable in the correct orientation.
5. Replace the system unit cover.
6. Plug in and start your PC, restoring the previous CMOS settings.

WHAT YOU NEED TO KNOW

In this lesson, you learned how to recognize when your CMOS battery has failed and how to replace it.

In the next lesson you will learn about IRQ conflicts. When you install a new hardware card, you might need to specify the board's IRQ setting. IRQ is an abbreviation for interrupt request. Each card you insert must have a unique IRQ number. If two boards have the same IRQ setting, the boards will not work. Lesson 8 examines steps you can perform to avoid such conflicts. Before you continue with Lesson 8, make sure that you understand the following key concepts:

✓ When the PC's power is off, the PC uses a special battery-powered CMOS memory to remember key system settings.

✓ Over time, the CMOS battery will fail and you must replace it.

✓ If your CMOS battery has failed, you will be notified when you start your computer.

✓ There are two types of CMOS batteries: one that looks like a nickel and one that looks like a battery pack.

✓ After you replace the CMOS battery, you must restore the previous CMOS settings.

Section Two

COMMON MOTHERBOARD UPGRADES

The PC's motherboard houses the majority of your computer's chips and circuits. In particular, you will find your computer's processor (the CPU or central processing unit) and random access memory (RAM) on the motherboard. The lessons in this section examine several upgrades you can make to items found on the motherboard and include the following:

Lesson 8 Understanding Common Conflicts

Lesson 9 Understanding DIP Switches and Jumpers

Lesson 10 Upgrading Your Processor

Lesson 11 Upgrading the PC BIOS

Lesson 12 Adding a Math Coprocessor

Lesson 13 Adding Memory to Your PC

Lesson 8

Understanding Common Conflicts

When you install a hardware card, such as a modem, mouse, or network adapter, you will need to assign settings to the card, such as the interrupt request line (IRQ), a memory buffer, and possibly a direct memory access (DMA) address. To avoid hardware conflicts, which prevent your system from working, each card within your computer must have unique settings.

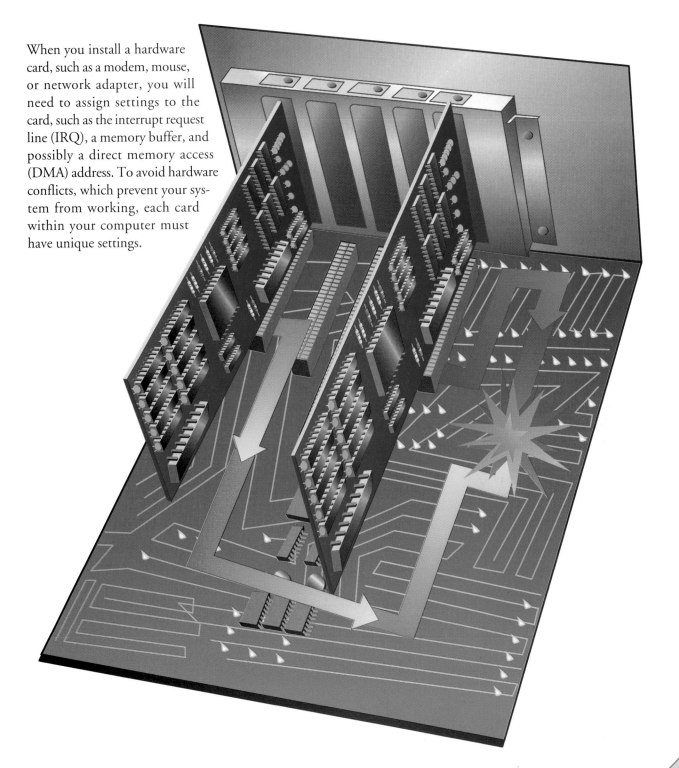

This lesson examines the steps you must perform to determine the correct settings and then to assign the settings. By the time you finish this lesson, you will understand the following key concepts:

- The purpose of an interrupt request (IRQ)
- How to determine available IRQ settings
- How to set a card's IRQ
- The purpose of a card's I/O address
- How to set a card's I/O address
- The purpose of a card's memory address
- How to set a card's memory address
- The purpose of direct memory access (DMA)
- How to assign a card's DMA setting

Selecting the correct settings for a card is one of the most difficult steps to installing a new card. If the settings you select are already in use by a different card, your computer may behave erratically, or it might not work at all.

UNDERSTANDING INTERRUPT REQUESTS

Within your computer, the central processing unit (CPU) oversees all operations. As your CPU runs a program, there will be times when a device such as a modem or mouse needs the CPU's attention. In such cases, the device *interrupts* the CPU so the CPU can perform special processing for the device. For example, each time you move your mouse across your desk, the mouse notifies the CPU so the CPU can move the mouse cursor across your screen display and update the screen. When the CPU completes the special processing, the CPU resumes the task it was performing prior to the interrupt.

Note: Every time you move the mouse, the CPU is interrupted from the task it was performing while it figures out where you are moving the mouse and adjusts the screen display of the cursor appropriately. This consumes significant amounts of CPU time. If you are waiting for a process to complete, try to refrain from wiggling the mouse to amuse yourself (a common temptation), and the process will go faster.

UNDERSTANDING INTERRUPTS

When a device interrupts the CPU, it submits an *interrupt request* or *IRQ*, whereupon the CPU stops working on its current task and performs special processing for the device. When the special processing is complete, the CPU resumes its previous operation.

Assume, for example, you are watching a video on TV and the phone rings. So you don't miss any part of the movie, you can pause the movie before you answer the phone (your interruption). When you have finished with the phone call, you can start the movie right where you left off. Wiggling the mouse while you wait for a process to complete is like receiving extra phone calls—the process takes longer.

Because many different devices can interrupt the CPU, the CPU needs a way to determine which device is causing the interrupt. Thus, each device has its own *interrupt request line*.

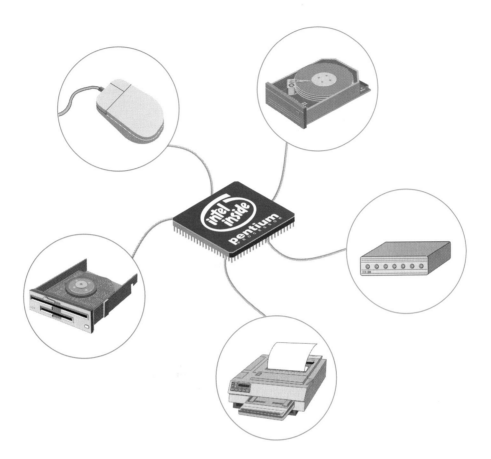

If you are using an older PC based on an eight-bit bus (see Lesson 4), your system will support eight IRQ lines, numbered 0 through 7. Table 8.1 lists the devices that normally correspond to these IRQ lines.

IRQ Number	Device
0	Timer
1	Keyboard
2	Available for use
3	COM2
4	COM1
5	Hard disk controller
6	Floppy disk controller
7	LPT1

Table 8.1 Devices that normally correspond to IRQ 0 through 7 on an eight-bit bus.

If you are using a 286-based PC or higher, your system will use 16 IRQ lines, numbered 0 through 15. Table 8.2 lists the devices normally assigned to these IRQ lines.

IRQ Number	Device	IRQ Number	Device
0	Timer	8	Real time clock
1	Keyboard	9	Redirected as IRQ2
2	Cascaded	10	Available for use
3	COM2	11	Available for use
4	COM1	12	Available for use
5	LPT2	13	Math coprocessor
6	Floppy disk controller	14	Hard disk controller
7	LPT1	15	Available for use

Table 8.2 *Devices normally associated with IRQ 0 though 15.*

To support the 16 IRQ levels, PCs use two special chips called *interrupt controllers*. The first controller chip corresponds to interrupts 0 through 7 and the second to interrupts 8 through 15. To access this second set of interrupts, PCs actually steal the line for IRQ 2 and use it for a special purpose. To activate one of the interrupts on the second controller, the PC sends a signal on IRQ 2. In this way, IRQ 2 is said to be *cascaded*. When a signal is sent on IRQ 2, the second interrupt controller jumps into action. Thus, your (286-based or higher) PC really only supports 15 interrupt request lines.

If you examine different hardware cards, such as a modem or a mouse, for example, you might find that the card's default setting is IRQ 2. As you just learned, however, IRQ 2 is not really used. When you set a card to IRQ 2, it is transparently routed to IRQ 9. In Lesson 36 you will learn how to use the MSD command to determine available IRQ settings. If you examine the MSD IRQ Status dialog box, you may find that IRQ 2 is set to something called *Second 8259A*—that's the second interrupt controller. If you examine IRQ 9, you will see that it corresponds to the *Redirected IRQ 2*. Figure 8.1, for example, illustrates a sample MSD IRQ Status screen. When you need to assign an IRQ to a new device, search the MSD screen for a *(Reserved)* entry. These entries correspond to available IRQs.

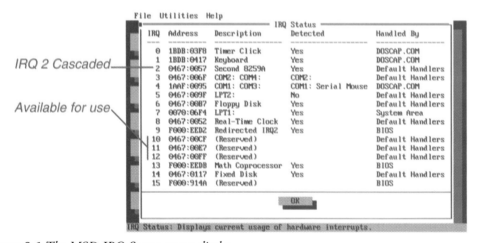

Figure 8.1 *The MSD IRQ Status screen display.*

QUICKLY LOCATING AVAILABLE IRQS

When you install a new hardware card, you might need to assign an IRQ (interrupt request) line to the card. Each card in your system must have a unique IRQ. To determine an available IRQ, perform these steps:

1. Invoke the MSD command from the DOS prompt (type **MSD**).

2. Press **Q** to select the IRQ Settings option.

3. From the list of IRQs, search for a (Reserved) entry. These entries are available for use.

SETTING A CARD'S INTERRUPT REQUEST

When you purchase a hardware card, the card will come with a preselected IRQ. If you examine the card, you will find a jumper or DIP switch that selects the IRQ setting.

Before you install the card, use the MSD command, discussed in Lesson 36, to determine your PC's current IRQ use. If the IRQ setting assigned to your card is not currently in use, you can install your card. If the IRQ setting is in use, change the jumper or DIP switches to change the IRQ setting to one that is not in use. Remember, if two cards have the same IRQ setting, the cards, and possibly your computer, will not work.

UNDERSTANDING A CARD'S I/O ADDRESS

In addition to using an IRQ, many cards also use a specific three-digit (hexadecimal) address often called the *port address* or *I/O address*. These special address values correspond to memory locations that are contained on the card itself. For example, when a program needs to send a character out of a serial port such as COM1, the program places the character into a special port address on the serial card. Each card uses a unique port address.

Normally, you will not need to change a board's I/O address. However, if, after you install a card, the card or possibly another card quits working, you should examine both cards to check for an I/O address conflict. Should you need to change a card's port address, you will change a jumper or DIP switch, as previously shown.

UNDERSTANDING A CARD'S MEMORY ADDRESS

As you just learned, many cards perform I/O operations using small memory locations (that reside on the card) called ports. Depending on your card type, the card may require a range of bytes in the PC's upper-memory region as well. The upper-memory region is the 384Kb range of memory that resides between the PC's 640Kb conventional memory and extended memory.

Most of the upper-memory region is used by your video card to hold the image currently displayed on the screen. However, part of the region is not used. Thus, devices that need to transfer larger amounts of data may reserve a portion of this unused memory. In such cases, you might have to specify the base or starting address for the device's memory range.

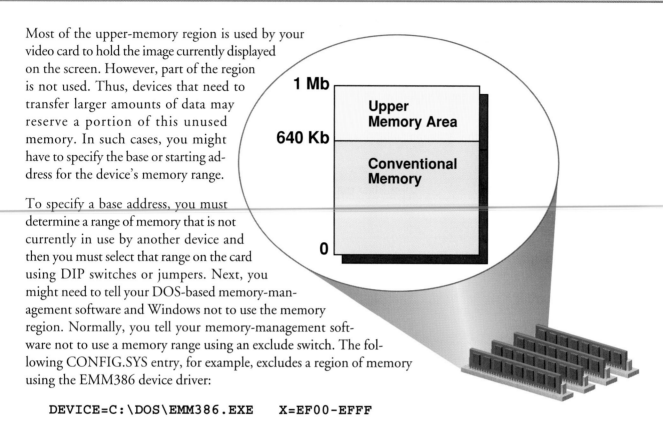

To specify a base address, you must determine a range of memory that is not currently in use by another device and then you must select that range on the card using DIP switches or jumpers. Next, you might need to tell your DOS-based memory-management software and Windows not to use the memory region. Normally, you tell your memory-management software not to use a memory range using an exclude switch. The following CONFIG.SYS entry, for example, excludes a region of memory using the EMM386 device driver:

```
DEVICE=C:\DOS\EMM386.EXE   X=EF00-EFFF
```

As you can see, the memory addresses used are in hexadecimal. The documentation that accompanied your card should include instructions for excluding memory in this way. If you are using Windows, you might need to place an EMMExclude statement within your SYSTEM.INI file as follows:

```
EMMExclude=EF00-EFFF
```

Admittedly, excluding a memory region for a card's use can be a challenging task. If you have difficulties, contact the card's technical support staff or a local PC user group and ask for help.

UNDERSTANDING DIRECT MEMORY ACCESS

As information flows through your computer, the information normally moves under the watchful eye of your computer's CPU. For example, if a program wants to display an image on the screen, the CPU moves the image into the computer's video memory. Although the CPU is well equipped to move information in this way, there are times when using the CPU as a "data mover" is a waste of the CPU's time. For example, when a program reads information from disk, the disk will normally transfer a sector of data (usually 512 bytes) to the computer's memory. Rather than having the CPU transfer the data, a special chip, called a *direct memory access* chip, oversees the operation, letting the CPU work on other tasks.

The term *DMA* is used to describe the process of moving data to or from memory without the need of the CPU. During a DMA operation, data flows down wires called a *DMA channel*. If you are using a 286-based PC or higher, the PC uses two DMA controllers with seven DMA channels, as listed in Table 8.3.

DMA Channel Number	Channel Use
0	Eight-bit data transfers
1	Eight-bit data transfers
2	Floppy disk transfers
3	Eight-bit data transfers
4	Cascade for DMA channels 0 through 3
5	16-bit data transfers
6	16-bit data transfers

Table 8.3 *DMA channel use within the PC.*

When you install a DMA device into your PC, you might need to select a DMA channel using DIP switches and jumpers. Normally, two devices that use DMA will not conflict unless, for some reason, both devices try to perform a DMA operation at the same time. If you install a device that uses DMA and you begin to encounter intermittent errors, you might need to check your device's DMA channel settings.

WHAT YOU NEED TO KNOW

In this lesson, you have learned about IRQ settings, port addresses, memory regions, and DMA channels, all of which must be set properly for the devices that use them to work properly.

When you install a new hardware board, there will be times when you need to change one or more board settings. To change a board setting, you will normally use jumpers and DIP switches, as you will learn in Lesson 9. Before you continue with Lesson 9, however, make sure that you understand the following key concepts.

- ✓ When you install a card and the card or PC fails to work, you might have a hardware conflict. Common hardware conflicts occur with IRQ settings, I/O addresses, memory regions, and DMA channels.

- ✓ Each card you install in your system uses a unique interrupt request (IRQ) to ask the CPU to perform special processing on its behalf. To set a card's IRQ, you use jumpers or DIP switches that reside on the card.

- ✓ To determine available IRQ settings, use the MSD command.

- ✓ An I/O address, or port address, is a special memory location built into the card itself that can be used for small input and output operations or to set various card settings. Most cards use a three-digit (hexadecimal) port address.

- ✓ If a card needs to work with larger amounts of data, the card may request a range of memory from the PC's upper-memory region. If a card uses such memory, you must exclude the memory region from being used by your DOS-based memory manager or Windows.

- ✓ Direct memory access is a technique that lets a special controller chip transfer large amounts of data from a device into the computer's memory without the use of the CPU as a "data mover." Devices that use DMA may require that you assign them to a specific DMA channel.

Lesson 9

Understanding DIP Switches and Jumpers

Within your computer, boards communicate with the processor by sending electronic signals. To let the processor know which board is signaling it, each board is assigned unique addresses and interrupt request lines (IRQs). Lesson 8 discussed several of these settings in detail. When you install a hardware board, such as an internal modem or sound card, there may be times when you need to change the board's hardware settings to avoid conflicts with an existing board within your computer. To change a board's settings, you must change one or more DIP switches or one or more jumpers, both of which are found on the board. This lesson examines DIP switches and jumpers. By the time you finish this lesson, you will understand the following key concepts:

- How to locate jumpers and DIP switches

- How to set DIP switches

- How to change jumper settings

Hardware boards use jumpers and DIP switches for many different purposes. The documentation that accompanies the board will describe their use in detail.

Don't let jumpers and DIP switches intimidate you. As you will learn in this lesson, they are actually very easy to use. As the number of hardware boards you install in your system increases, you will eventually need to change a jumper or DIP switch setting.

WORKING WITH *DIP* SWITCHES

The term DIP is an acronym for dual inline package, which describes how the switch components were designed. *DIP switches* look like a miniature collection of light switches.

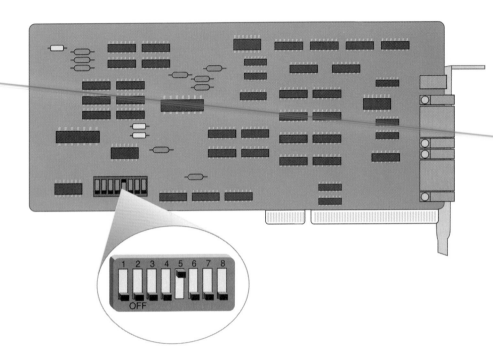

If you examine a DIP switch closely, you will find that the switches are labeled On/Off, Open/Closed, or 1/0.

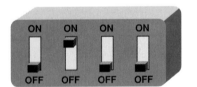  

Hardware boards use DIP switches for many different purposes. In fact, a board may have several DIP switches. If you examine your hardware board closely, you will find that each switch has a unique number, such as switch 1 or switch 2.

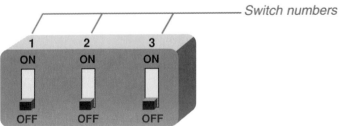

As you read the documentation that accompanies your board, you might be instructed to change a specific switch setting. Never change a DIP switch setting without first writing down the original settings.

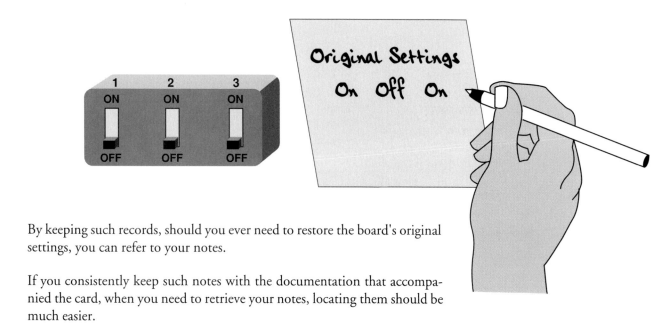

By keeping such records, should you ever need to restore the board's original settings, you can refer to your notes.

If you consistently keep such notes with the documentation that accompanied the card, when you need to retrieve your notes, locating them should be much easier.

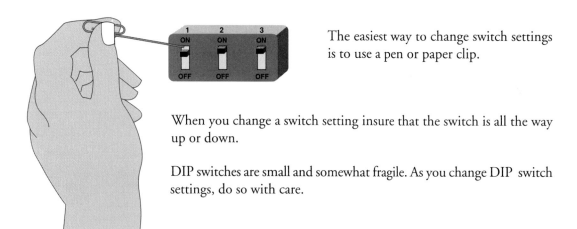

The easiest way to change switch settings is to use a pen or paper clip.

When you change a switch setting insure that the switch is all the way up or down.

DIP switches are small and somewhat fragile. As you change DIP switch settings, do so with care.

UNDERSTANDING DIP SWITCHES

DIP switches provide one way for you to change (or configure) a hardware board. Depending on the board, two or more switches may be present. Most hardware boards clearly label each switch. The documentation that accompanies your hardware board will explain the purpose of each switch. The easiest way to change a switch is to use a pen or paper clip.

Note: Never change DIP settings without first writing down the original switch settings.

WORKING WITH JUMPERS

Jumpers provide a second way to configure a hardware board. Jumpers let you physically connect two electrical pins, completing an electrical path. When you remove a jumper, you open (turn off) the path.

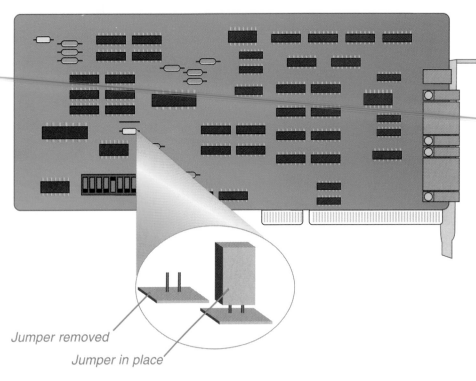

Jumper removed

Jumper in place

Like DIP switches, a hardware board can have two or more jumpers. If you examine the board closely, you will find that each jumper has a unique number, such as jumper 1 or jumper 2. The documentation that accompanies your board will define each jumper's purpose.

As was the case with DIP switches, never change jumper settings without first recording the original state. Also, should you remove a jumper, place the connector in a safe location.

In many cases, users leave the jumper connected to one pin. In this way, the jumper connector does not complete a connection but it also does not get lost.

Note: *You should never change a jumper setting without writing down the original settings.*

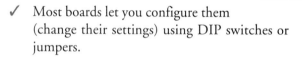

In some cases you can easily remove or add jumpers using only your fingers. In other cases, you will need to use needlenose pliers.

When using pliers, gently grip the jumper's center, sliding the jumper on or off.

WHAT YOU NEED TO KNOW

In this lesson, you learned that, as you install more hardware boards, the likelihood that two or more will request the same address or interrupt line increases. These boards use DIP switches or jumpers to let you switch the settings to an available memory location or request line.

In anticipation of Intel's Pentium processor, many 486-based computers were designed to have their 486 processor upgraded to a Pentium. In Lesson 10 you will learn how to upgrade such "Pentium-ready" systems. Likewise, you can now also replace many 386 processors with a 486 by simply replacing chips! Before you continue with Lesson 10, however, make sure that you understand the following key concepts:

✓ Most boards let you configure them (change their settings) using DIP switches or jumpers.

✓ A DIP switch is a small, normally plastic, group of switches. Using a paper clip, you can turn individual switches on or off to change the board's configuration.

✓ A jumper is a small connector that you slide over two pins to complete a circuit connection or that you remove to break a circuit. By changing the board's circuitry using jumpers, you change the board's configuration.

✓ Never change DIP switch or jumper settings without first writing down the original settings.

Lesson 10

Upgrading Your Processor

Historically, when a new PC processor ships, such as the Pentium, the processor's first-year prices are quite high. As a rule, if you can delay your upgrade 12 to 18 months, you will save considerable money. With the knowledge that many users often delay their processor upgrades, many PC manufacturers now sell PCs that are processor upgradeable. In the case of the Pentium processor, for example, these upgradeable PCs are often classified as "Pentium ready." This lesson examines the steps you must perform to upgrade your processor. By the time you finish this lesson, you will understand the following key concepts:

- The difference between the Pentium processor and a 486

- The steps you must perform to install a Pentium

- How you can upgrade your 386 to a 486

You cannot plug a Pentium processor into just any PC. Instead, your PC's motherboard must be designed to accept the Pentium. In other words, your motherboard must be *Pentium ready*. If your 486 is not Pentium ready, you may be able to increase your system performance by replacing your processor with an Intel OverDrive processor. Using the OverDrive processor, your system should run as much as 1 1/2 times faster.

What You'll Need

Before you get started with this lesson, make sure that you have the following readily available:

1. A PC tool kit with a screwdriver.
2. A container within which you can place the chassis screws.
3. A well-lit workspace with room for you to place the chassis.
4. A new processor.

Note: Before you begin, make sure that you are working in a static-free environment. Also, ground yourself by touching your system unit chassis before you touch a processor chip.

How the Pentium Differs from a 486

Depending on the programs you run, the Pentium processor, the newest offering from Intel, can run up to five times as fast as a 66MHz 486! When processor designers try to improve a processor's performance, they focus their efforts on the three following techniques:

- Increase the number of transistors on the processor chip
- Increase the processor chip's clock speed
- Increase the number of instructions per clock cycle

Computers execute programs by sending electronic signals from one component to another. By increasing the number of transistors in the processor chip, the Pentium allows more components to be placed within the processor itself. As a result, signals aren't sent as far and their transfer times are reduced. By reducing signal transfer times, the Pentium improves its performance. The 486 supports 1,250,000 transistors. The Pentium, on the other hand, supports over three million. Table 10.1 lists the number of transistors in PC processors over the years.

Processor Type	Number of Transistors
8088	30,000
80286	130,000
80386	250,000
80486	1,250,000
Pentium	3,000,000

Table 10.1 The number of transistors in different PC processor types.

Within the CPU, operations are controlled using a single *clock*, which keeps the computer's electronic components in synch. Each click of the clock is called a *clock cycle*. In the original IBM PC ,which released in 1981, the clock ticked 4.7 million times per second. In the Pentium, like most 486s, the clock ticks 66 million times per second.

Note: As you shop for PCs, you will encounter different processor speeds, some faster or slower than 66MHz. Keep in mind that the faster the processor, the faster the PC.

A program is a list of instructions that the CPU executes. In the past, processors normally executed a single instruction with one or more clock ticks. The Pentium, however, is now capable of executing two instructions per clock tick. By combining these three techniques, Pentium processors are able to execute over 100 million instructions per second!

A TRANSISTOR IS A CHIP'S WORKHORSE

As electronic signals flow through the computer, devices need a way to store or hold signals. When computers were first built in the 1940s, the computers used vacuum tubes. Because the vacuum tubes were very large, hot, and subject to failure, the transistor was designed. Transistors are so named because they transmit signals across a resistor.

Computer chips (sometimes called integrated circuits) are collections of many transistors. As Table 10.2 shows, chips are categorized by the number of transistors they contain.

Transistor Count	Chip Classification	Category
1 to 500	Small- to medium-scale integration	SSI or MSI
501 to 10,000	Large-scale integration	LSI
10,001 to 100,000	Very-large-scale integration	VLSI
Over 100,000	Ultra-large-scale integration	ULSI

Table 10.2 Chip classification by transistor count.

INSTALLING A PENTIUM PROCESSOR

To install a Pentium processor, power off and unplug your PC. Next, remove the PC's system unit cover, as discussed in Lesson 2. Locate your current processor on the motherboard. Your processor chip will likely be labeled with the number 486.

Note: Don't forget to discharge any static charge that your body may have accumulated before touching any chips. You can discharge such static by simply touching your system chassis.

To simplify the removal and insertion of processor chips, many motherboards use a ZIF or zero-insertion-force processor socket. To remove the processor from a ZIF socket, simply raise up the socket lever. The processor chip should rise to the top of the socket.

To insert the Pentium processor into the ZIF socket, gently align the processor's pins into the socket and close the socket lever. The processor will slide gently and securely into place. The ZIF socket is so named because you apply no (zero) force to insert the chip into the socket.

Note: When you are replacing any chip, make certain that the replacement is pointing the same way as the original.

Replace and secure your PC's system unit cover. Next, plug in and power on your PC. When your PC starts, it will be using the Pentium processor!

INSTALLING A PENTIUM PROCESSOR

To install a Pentium processor into a Pentium-ready PC, follow these steps:

1. Power off and unplug the PC system unit.
2. Remove the system unit cover, as discussed in Lesson 2, and discharge any static from your body.
3. Locate the current processor chip on the motherboard and remove it.
4. Insert the Pentium processor chip into the socket.
5. Replace the system unit cover.
6. Plug in and power on the PC system unit.

UPGRADING A 386 TO A 486

If you are using a 386-based PC, you can now upgrade your PC by replacing the processor chip. If you examine PC magazines, you will find processors, such as the Cyrix 486, that can be plugged directly into a 386 processor slot. In this way, you can upgrade your 386 to a 486 in a matter of minutes! Depending on the processor you buy, the steps you must perform to replace the processor may differ slightly. In general, however, you can follow the guidelines just discussed for the Pentium upgrade.

WHAT YOU NEED TO KNOW

In this lesson you learned that you may be able to upgrade your 486 to a Pentium or your 386 to a 486 with one simple operation. Upgrading the processor is the biggest single thing most users can do to speed up their computers.

When your computer performs keyboard input, writes to the screen display, or reads or writes files on disk, your computer normally uses a special chip called the BIOS (Basic Input Output System). Depending on the age of your PC, there may be times when you need to replace the BIOS. In Lesson 11 you will examine the steps required to replace the BIOS. Before you continue with Lesson 11, however, make sure that you have learned the following key concepts:

✓ The Pentium is a processor chip capable of running five times faster than a 66MHz 486.

✓ The Pentium improves its performance by integrating more transistors, over three million, and by increasing the number of instructions it can execute in a single clock tick.

✓ You may be able to upgrade your 386 processor to a 486 simply by replacing the processor chip.

✓ You cannot install a Pentium processor into any 486-based PC. Instead, the PC must be "Pentium ready."

Lesson 11

Upgrading the PC BIOS

The PC BIOS is a pair of computer chips that oversees all input and output operations. When programs read keystrokes from the keyboard or display text or pictures to the screen display, the programs rely on the BIOS chips. In addition, the BIOS oversees disk I/O and other key operations. BIOS is an acronym for Basic Input/Output System.

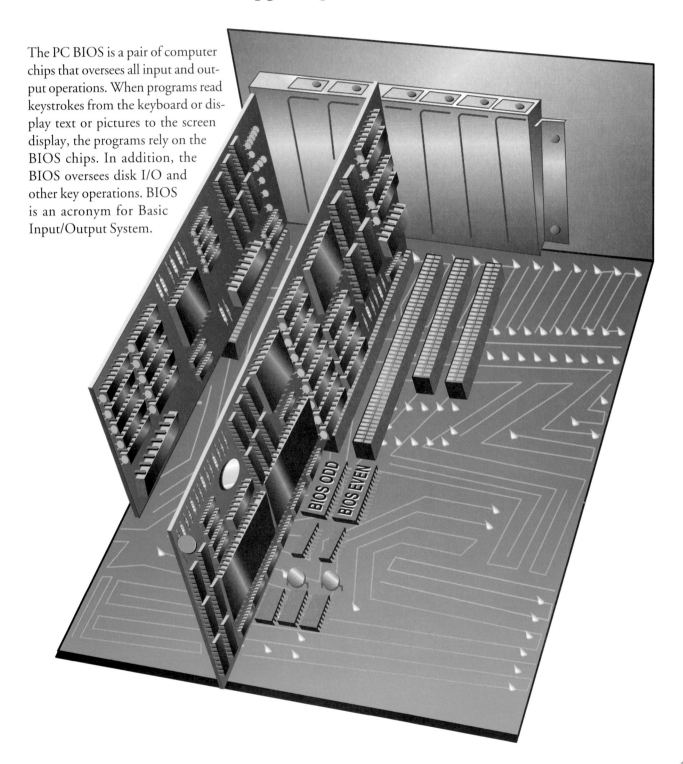

If you have an older PC, there may come a time when you need to upgrade your PC BIOS before you can use a new device. This lesson examines the steps you must perform to upgrade your PC BIOS. By the time you finish this lesson, you will understand the following key concepts:

- How you know when you need to upgrade the BIOS
- How replacing the BIOS can lead to compatibility problems
- How to replace the BIOS chips

WHAT YOU'LL NEED

Before you get started with this lesson, make sure that you have the following readily available:

1. A PC tool kit with a screwdriver and chip extractor.
2. A container within which you can place the chassis screws.
3. A well-lit workspace with room for you to place the chassis.
4. New, compatible BIOS chips.

Note: Before you begin, make sure that you are working in a static-free environment. Also ground yourself by touching your system unit chassis before you touch a BIOS chip.

How You Know When You Need to Replace Your BIOS

Most users will never upgrade their PC BIOS because, quite frankly, they'll have no reason to do so. Normally, the need to update your BIOS occurs when you install a new floppy disk or other BIOS-based device into an older system. When the device does not work, an often overlooked cause is incompatibility between the device and BIOS. Users normally don't intentionally set out to upgrade their BIOS. Instead, an incompatibility forces the upgrade.

Some users might suggest that replacing an older BIOS is a good way to improve your system performance. Although newer BIOS chips may indeed be faster, they might not be compatible with your system. In such cases, the net result is a fast system that does not work. Before you upgrade your BIOS, always check with your PC manufacturer first to ensure that the BIOS upgrade is compatible with your system.

UNDERSTANDING THE PC BIOS

The PC BIOS is a pair of computer chips that oversees input and output operations. To upgrade the BIOS, you simply replace the chips with new ones. Most users never have a need to upgrade the BIOS. Before you upgrade your BIOS, check with your PC manufacturer to ensure that the BIOS upgrade is compatible with your system.

Keep in mind that most users normally don't upgrade their BIOS chips to improve their system performance. Instead, users upgrade the BIOS to gain support for a new device.

Upgrading Your System BIOS

After you ensure that the new BIOS is fully compatible with your system, power off and unplug the PC's system unit. Next, remove the system unit cover as discussed in Lesson 2.

Locate the BIOS chips on the motherboard. Before you touch the BIOS chips, make sure you discharge static electricity by grounding yourself to your system chassis.

The BIOS uses a pair of chips—one called *odd* and one *even*. When you replace the chips, you must place the odd and even chips in the correct sockets. Stop now and make a note of the chip orientation.

Using a chip extractor, gently remove each BIOS chip from its socket, replacing the chip with the corresponding odd or even new chip.

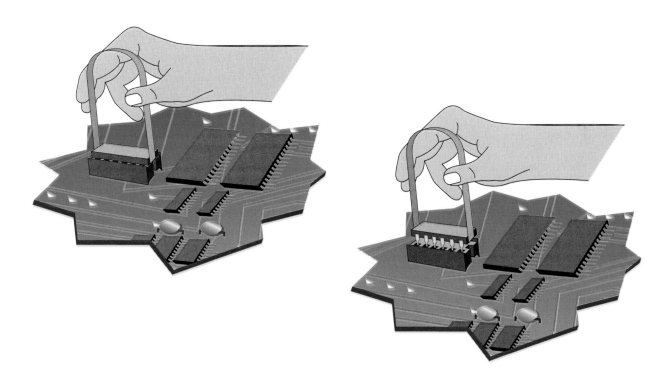

After you replace both chips, replace your system unit cover. Plug in and power on your PC. If you have installed the new BIOS chips correctly, your system will perform its power-on self-test. After your system starts, make sure you can access your disk drives and can perform screen and keyboard I/O.

Upgrading Your BIOS Chips

Before you purchase new BIOS chips, make sure the chips are fully compatible with your system. One way to increase the likelihood that your chips are compatible is to purchase the chips from the same manufacturer who built your PC.

To change your BIOS chips, perform these steps:

1. Power off and unplug your PC system unit.

2. Remove the system unit cover, as discussed in Lesson 2, and discharge static from your body.

3. Locate the pair of BIOS chips on the motherboard. Remove the chips from their sockets using a chip extractor.

4. Insert the new odd and even BIOS chips into the correct sockets.

5. Replace the system unit cover.

6. Plug in and power on your PC system unit.

Note: If your system does not start, verify that you have placed the odd and even BIOS chips into the correct sockets.

What You Need to Know

When you install a new hardware device into an older PC, the device might not be recognized by your PC BIOS (Basic Input/Output System). In this lesson, you learned how to upgrade your BIOS.

If you use your computer to run math-intensive programs, such as a computer-aided design (CAD) program, or to create complex spreadsheets, you might improve your system performance by adding a math coprocessor. Lesson 12 discusses which processors have a built-in math coprocessor and which do not. You will also learn how to decide if a math coprocessor will improve your system performance, and if so, how to install one. Before you continue with Lesson 12, however, make sure that you understand the following key concepts:

✓ BIOS is an acronym for Basic Input Output System. Your computer's BIOS is a pair of chips that oversee most input and output (I/O) operations.

✓ Most users do not upgrade their BIOS to improve their system performance. Instead, users upgrade the BIOS to obtain support for a new device.

✓ Before you upgrade your BIOS, you need to ensure that the new BIOS will be fully compatible with your system. One of the best sources to ask is your original PC manufacturer.

✓ BIOS chips come in pairs, one called the odd BIOS chip and one called the even. When you upgrade your BIOS chips, you need to ensure that you install the odd chip into the odd socket and the even chip into the even socket.

Lesson 12

Adding a Math Coprocessor

To run programs, your computer relies on its central processing unit, or CPU. The CPU is the computer's electronic brain, which oversees most operations. A computer program is simply a list of instructions the computer performs, much like a recipe is a set of instructions a cook performs. When you run a program, the CPU executes the program instructions. An instruction might tell the CPU to add two numbers, to move a value in memory, and so on.

In general, the CPU only executes simple instructions, such as adding two numbers. If a program needs to determine a value's square root or an angle's cosine, the program must break the operation into a series of more general instructions the CPU understands.

Depending on the operation, the number of instructions can become long and time consuming for the CPU to execute. To improve the PC's performance, many users add a special math coprocessor, which can execute arithmetic operations quickly. Like the CPU, a math coprocessor is a chip.

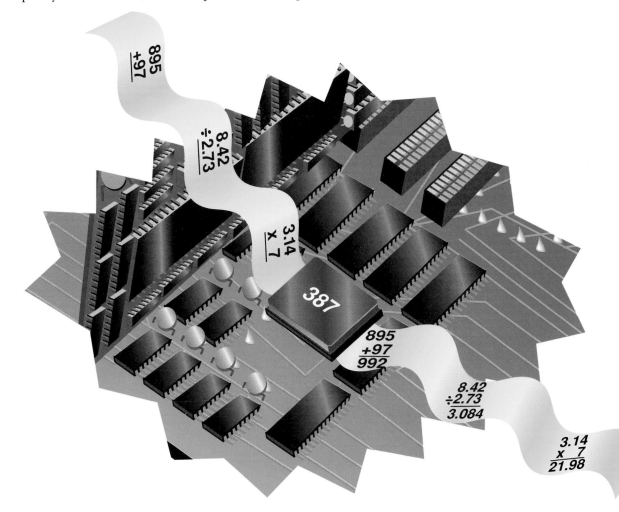

This lesson examines math coprocessors in detail. By the time you finish this lesson, you will understand the following key concepts:

- The purpose of a math coprocessor and whether or not the math coprocessor will improve your system performance

- How to determine if your PC already has a math coprocessor

- The steps you must perform to install a math coprocessor

WHAT YOU'LL NEED

Before you get started with this lesson, make sure that you have the following readily available:

1. A PC tool kit with a screwdriver.

2. A container within which you can place the chassis screws.

3. A well-lit workspace with room for you to place the chassis.

4. A new math coprocessor.

Note: Before you begin, make sure that you are working in a static-free environment. Also ground yourself by touching your system unit chassis before you touch a math coprocessor chip.

UNDERSTANDING THE MATH COPROCESSOR

A *math coprocessor* is a computer chip specifically designed to perform arithmetic operations quickly. If you use your computer to perform number-crunching applications, such as a spreadsheet, CAD, or scientific program, a math coprocessor should improve your system performance. On the other hand, if you normally just run word processor or database programs, the math coprocessor won't improve your system performance. Such programs normally don't perform complex arithmetic operations. Thus, the math coprocessor is not used.

WILL A MATH COPROCESSOR IMPROVE YOUR SYSTEM PERFORMANCE

A math coprocessor is a specialized computer chip that can perform arithmetic operations quickly. If you use your computer to run spreadsheets, scientific, or engineering programs, a math coprocessor should improve your system performance. If, however, you only use your computer to run Windows or for word processing, however, a math coprocessor will not improve your system performance.

DETERMINING WHETHER YOUR PC NEEDS A MATH COPROCESSOR

In the past, if you were using a 386-based PC or older, you had to buy and install a math coprocessor. Newer CPUs such as the Pentium and *some* 486s, however, have a built-in math coprocessor. One of the easiest ways to determine if your PC has a math coprocessor is to use the MSD (Microsoft Diagnostic) command provided with DOS 6 and Windows. Lesson 36 examines the MSD command in detail. For now, run MSD from the DOS prompt, as shown here:

```
C:\> MSD  <ENTER>
```

MSD will display its main menu, as shown in Figure 12.1.

Figure 12.1 The MSD main menu.

Press **P** to select MSD's Computer option. MSD will display the Computer dialog box, as shown in Figure 12.2, which states whether or not a math coprocessor is present.

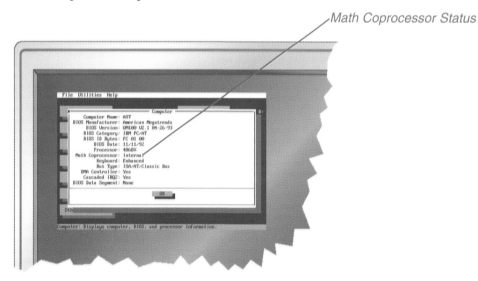

Figure 12.2 The MSD Computer dialog box.

Press **ENTER** to remove the dialog box. Next, press **ALT-F** to select MSD's File menu and choose the Exit option. If your PC already has a math coprocessor, you can continue your reading with Lesson 13.

SHOPPING FOR A MATH COPROCESSOR

As you know, the computer's CPU type is identified by a unique number, such as a 286 or 386. When you purchase a math coprocessor, you must match the CPU type. Math coprocessors are identified by similar numbers, such as a 287 or 387, to facilitate proper matching.

If you are using a 486, however, things get a little more difficult. If you examine advertisements for 486 computers, you will find 486DX and 486SX processors. As it turns out, 486DX processors have a built-in math coprocessor and 486SX processors do not. As a result, 486DX computers tend to be more expensive.

When you price a 487 math coprocessor, you may find it is more expensive than its 287 and 387 counterparts. As it turns out, the 487 math coprocessor is actually a 486 with a built-in math coprocessor. In other words, it is almost identical to the 486DX processor. The difference between the 486DX and the 487 is simply an extra pin that prevents the chips from being plug compatible. When you install the 487, it takes over all processing, and the original 486SX becomes idle.

INSTALLING A MATH COPROCESSOR

To install a math coprocessor, turn off and unplug your PC. Next, open your system unit, as discussed in Lesson 2, and free yourself of all static charge. If you examine your motherboard, you will find a coprocessor socket very close to your processor socket. You might need to refer to the documentation that accompanied your PC to locate the coprocessor socket.

Align the coprocessor pins to the socket and gently slide the coprocessor into place. Replace and secure your system unit cover and power on your PC. After your system starts, run the MSD command, as before. If your PC does not see the math coprocessor, access your PC's setup program and change your PC's CMOS settings, as discussed in Lesson 6.

Coprocessor Socket

INSTALLING A MATH COPROCESSOR

A math coprocessor is an easy upgrade that can improve the performance of application programs that perform complex arithmetic calculations. To install a math coprocessor, perform these steps:

1. Turn off and unplug your PC.

2. Open your system unit, placing the screws in a safe location, and discharge any static charge.

3. Locate the math coprocessor socket and gently insert the chip into the socket.

4. Replace and secure your system unit cover. Plug in and power on your PC.

5. After your system starts, run MSD to verify that the PC sees the math coprocessor. If the PC does not see the coprocessor, you might need to change your computer's CMOS settings.

WHAT YOU NEED TO KNOW

In this lesson, you learned how you can speed up CAD or other math-intensive programs by adding a math coprocessor.

As the size and complexity of programs continue to increase, so too does your need to add memory to your system. If you make extensive use of Windows, you will be amazed by how much faster your system runs if you use at least 8Mb of RAM. Lesson 13 discusses the steps you need to perform to add memory to your computer. Before you continue with Lesson 13, however, make sure that you have learned the following key concepts:

✓ A math coprocessor is a chip specifically designed to perform arithmetic operations. If you run math-intensive programs, adding a math coprocessor should improve your system performance.

✓ Math coprocessors have numbers that match the processors they go with.

✓ The math coprocessor usually sits in a socket near the processor.

✓ Some processors have a math coprocessor built in. The best way to determine if your system has a math coprocessor is to use the MSD command.

✓ If your computer does not recognize your newly installed math coprocessor, you might have to set the CMOS setting.

Lesson 13

Adding Memory to Your PC

As you have learned, a program (software) is simply a list of instructions the computer performs. Before your computer can run a program, the program must reside in your computer's random access memory (RAM). As programs become more powerful, they also become larger, requiring more RAM. Further, if you use Windows, you may have several different programs running at the same time, each of which requires its own memory space. When Windows runs out of memory, it temporarily moves programs in and out of memory to the much slower disk to make room for the current application to run. Although swapping programs in and out of memory in this way lets Windows run multiple programs at the same time, the disk operations required during the swaps significantly slow your system performance.

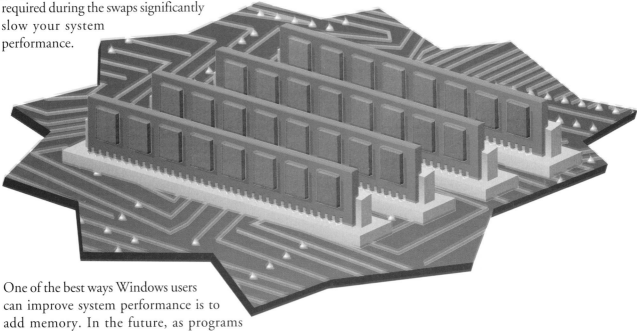

One of the best ways Windows users can improve system performance is to add memory. In the future, as programs become more complex or take advantage of multimedia video, 8Mb of RAM will become the standard, and fast systems will have more. This lesson examines the steps you must perform to add memory to your PC. By the time you finish this lesson, you will understand the following key concepts:

- How to determine how much memory your PC currently contains
- How to determine if adding memory will improve your system performance
- How to install SIMM chips
- After you install memory, you must tell your computer's CMOS

Normally, when you add memory to your system, you'll see immediate performance improvement. As such, everyone should consider adding more memory.

HOW MUCH MEMORY DO YOU HAVE

Before you make the decision to add more memory, you need to determine how much memory you already have. One of the easiest ways to find out how much memory your system contains is to issue the MEM command from the DOS prompt, as shown here:

```
C:\> MEM    <ENTER>

Memory Type        Total   =   Used   +   Free
_____        _____       ____       ____

Conventional        640K        48K        592K
Upper               155K       155K          0K
Reserved            128K       128K          0K
Extended (XMS)    7,269K     6,245K      1,024K
_____       _____     _____      _____

Total memory      8,192K     6,576K      1,616K

Total under 1 MB    795K       203K        592K

Largest executable program size       592K (605,696 bytes)
Largest free upper memory block         0K      (0 bytes)
MS-DOS is resident in the high memory area.
```

Next, before you add memory, evaluate how you use your PC. If you normally run multiple programs from within Windows, you will improve your system performance by adding memory. However, if you only run one program at a time from DOS, you probably won't see a tremendous performance improvement by adding more memory.

WILL ADDING MEMORY IMPROVE YOUR SYSTEM PERFORMANCE?

If you make extensive use of Windows and you normally have multiple programs running at the same time, adding memory to your system will improve your performance. If, however, you work from the DOS environment, you might not see a great change in performance by adding memory.

LOCATING YOUR SYSTEM MEMORY

PC memory resides on your system's motherboard. To locate your system's memory, first power off and unplug your PC.

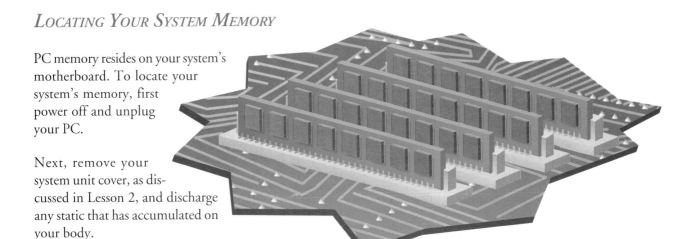

Next, remove your system unit cover, as discussed in Lesson 2, and discharge any static that has accumulated on your body.

Your computer's random access memory uses upright chips, called *SIMMs*. SIMM is an acronym for *single inline memory module*. In short, the term refers to the fact that several memory chips are stored in the same module, in line, as shown.

Note: If your computer is one of the minority that uses non-SIMM memory (you should be able to tell by looking), read your documentation or contact the manufacturer or the vendor that sold you the machine.

Locate the SIMM chips on your motherboard. Also, note the number of unused SIMM sockets.

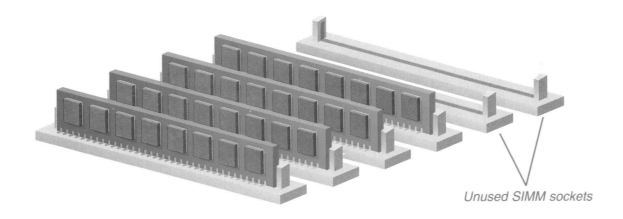

Unused SIMM sockets

Note: Before you begin, make sure that you are working in a static-free environment. Also ground yourself by touching your system unit chassis before you touch a processor chip.

WHAT TYPE OF SIMMs DO YOU NEED?

SIMM chips are sold as 1Mb, 2Mb, 4Mb, 8Mb, and so on—even up to 128Mb chips! However, your PC may only support 1Mb or 2Mb chips. Turn to the documentation that accompanied your PC or call your manufacturer's technical support to determine the size of memory your system can use.

In most cases, the SIMM memory size you add to your system must match the memory size your PC is currently using. In other words, if your PC contains 2Mb SIMMs, you probably can't add 4Mb chips. Instead, you must keep using 2Mb chips.

With the cost of SIMM chips constantly decreasing, you may find that if your PC supports larger SIMMs, you'll want to remove the smaller chips. For example, if the price of 4Mb chips becomes affordable and your system supports 4Mb chips, you may want to simply remove any 2Mb chips from your system.

Memory chips are classified by speed and size. Memory speed is expressed in terms of nanoseconds (ns), that is, billionths of seconds that a given task (such as a memory read) takes—the lower the number, the faster the chip. For example, you might buy 2Mb, 70ns SIMMs. Your system documentation will specify the minimum memory speed your system can use. As a rule, if you buy memory that is at least as fast as your system's current SIMM chips, you will be fine.

INSTALLING SIMM CHIPS

To add memory to your system, you simply insert a SIMM chip into the next available socket. Sounds easy right? In addition to the socket, PCs hold SIMMs in place using small notches that appear at the end of the socket.

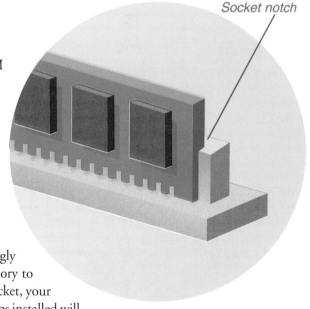

Socket notch

You need to be very careful when you insert the SIMM chip into these notches. If you break a notch off, the PC may not be able to hold the SIMM in place. As a result, the socket cannot be used and you cannot use other sockets! Worse yet— in many cases, the socket cannot be fixed!

Because an errant snap can have devastating results, I strongly recommend that you let your computer retailer add memory to your system for you. Should your retailer break a SIMM socket, your retailer is responsible. The money you spend having the chips installed will be much less than having to replace a motherboard because you have broken a SIMM socket.

Note: *If you choose to have your retailer install your SIMM chips for you, examine the chips before you leave the store to ensure that the retailer has not inadvertently broken a SIMM socket.*

If you choose to install a SIMM chip, you normally insert the chip into the slot at an angle, and then stand the chip upright, inserting the chip into notches that hold the chip in place.

INSTALL SIMM CHIPS WITH GREAT CARE

If you choose to install your own SIMM chips, do so with great care. When you install a SIMM chip, you slide the chip into the SIMM slot and then you snap the chip into notches that hold the chip in place. If you accidentally break one of these notches, you might not be able to use the SIMM socket or sockets that follow. New users might want their computer retailer to perform their SIMM upgrade for them.

To install SIMM chips, perform these steps:

1. Power off and unplug your PC system unit.

2. Open your system unit, as discussed in Lesson 2, and remove any static charge from your body by touching your system unit chassis.

3. Locate the unused SIMM slots.

4. Gently insert the SIMM chip into the next unused slot.

5. Replace and secure your system unit cover.

6. Plug in and power on your PC system unit.

MANY OLDER PCs USE MEMORY CARDS

Many older 286- and 386-based PCs do not use SIMM chips. Instead, the systems use a memory card.

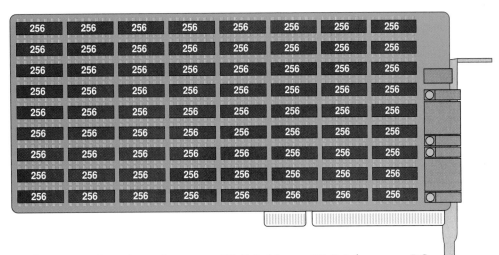

If you open your PC system unit and you do not see SIMM chips or SIMM slots, your PC may use card-based memory. In such cases, contact your PC retailer to determine the correct memory card type.

To install card-based memory, perform these steps:

1. Power off and unplug your PC system unit.

2. Open your system unit as discussed in Lesson 2, and free yourself of static.

3. Use the card's jumpers or DIP switches to configure the card's starting address, as discussed in the documentation that accompanies your card.

4. Locate an unused expansion slot and gently insert the card into the unused slot.

5. Replace and secure your system unit cover.

6. Plug in and power on your PC system unit.

TELLING YOUR SYSTEM ABOUT THE NEW MEMORY

After you install additional memory, you must tell your computer's CMOS about the new memory before you can put it to use. To inform the CMOS about the memory, access your CMOS setup program, as discussed in Lesson 6. Next, update the extended memory amount. Save your system settings and restart your system. If you are using Windows, turn to Lesson 23, which discusses how you fine-tune Windows memory use.

WHAT YOU NEED TO KNOW

It seems that you can never have too much RAM. In this lesson, you learned how to install more random access memory into your computer.

Many PCs only ship with a 5 1/4- or 3 1/2-inch drive, but not both. Thus, exchanging floppy disks with other users can be difficult. In Lesson 14 you will learn how to install a floppy disk in your system. In addition, you will learn about a popular dual floppy drive that includes a 5 1/4 and 3 1/2 drive in the same drive bay. Before you continue with Lesson 14, however, make sure that you have learned the following key concepts:

✓ A program is a list of instructions the computer executes. Before the computer can run a program, the program must reside within the computer's random access memory (RAM). Likewise, before a program can access data, such as a word processing document or a spread-sheet, the data must reside in memory.

✓ As programs become larger and more complex, their memory needs increase. In the future, as programs begin to make more use of multimedia video, sound, and pictures, your PC memory requirements will increase greatly.

✓ To determine how much memory your PC currently contains, you can use the DOS MEM command.

✓ You add memory to your PC (in most cases) by installing SIMM chips. When you shop for SIMMs, you need to know the size and speed you require. The documentation that accompanied your PC will specify the size chips your system supports, as well as the chip speed. In most cases, you cannot use two different sizes of SIMM chips. In other words, you cannot use 2Mb and 4Mb chips at the same time.

✓ The speed of a RAM chip is considered as a measure of access time, in nanoseconds (ns). The lower the number, the faster the chip. Choose replacements that are at least as fast as the originals.

✓ Not all PCs use SIMM chips. Instead, some older PCs use card-based memory. In such cases, you install the memory cards much like you would any expansion slot card.

✓ After you install memory chips within your system, you must inform your computer's CMOS of the change.

COMMON HARDWARE UPGRADES

When you think of upgrades, the first thing that comes to mind is hardware. The most spectacular upgrades, generally, are made by upgrading physical hardware, for example getting a new hard disk, CD-ROM, multimedia sound board, video card, monitor, floppy drive, modem, fax/modem, or printer. When you upgrade hardware, the results are immediate and visible. The lessons in this section show you when, why, and how to perform these upgrades. Once again, you can do this! The lessons presented in this section include the following:

Lesson 14 *Installing a Floppy Disk*

Lesson 15 *Installing a SCSI Adapter*

Lesson 16 *Installing a New Hard Drive*

Lesson 17 *Installing a Modem*

Lesson 18 *Installing a Multimedia Sound Card*

Lesson 19 *Upgrading Your Monitor*

Lesson 20 *Upgrading Your Video Card*

Lesson 21 *Installing a CD-ROM Drive*

Lesson 22 *Replacing the PC's Power Supply*

Lesson 23 *Upgrading Your Mouse*

Lesson 24 *Installing a Tape Backup Unit*

Lesson 25 *Upgrading Your Printer*

Lesson 26 *Upgrading Your Keyboard*

Lesson 27 *Basic Troubleshooting Tips*

Lesson 14

Installing a Floppy Disk

If your PC came with only a single 3 1/2- or 5 1/4-inch floppy disk drive, you might find it difficult to exchange files and disks with other users. In such cases, you can quickly and easily install a second floppy disk drive. Likewise, if you are adding a CD-ROM or tape drive and you must give up a drive bay in a crowded chassis, you might want to consider the half-height dual-floppy disk drive that combines a 3 1/2- and a 5 1/4-inch drive into one disk unit.

This lesson examines the steps you must perform to install a floppy disk drive. By the time you finish this lesson, you will understand the following key concepts:

- How to install and mount a floppy disk drive
- How to cable and power a floppy disk drive
- The advantages of using a dual-floppy drive

INSTALLING A FLOPPY DISK DRIVE

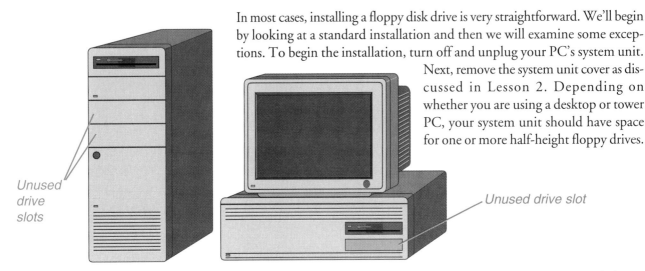

In most cases, installing a floppy disk drive is very straightforward. We'll begin by looking at a standard installation and then we will examine some exceptions. To begin the installation, turn off and unplug your PC's system unit. Next, remove the system unit cover as discussed in Lesson 2. Depending on whether you are using a desktop or tower PC, your system unit should have space for one or more half-height floppy drives.

Unused drive slots

Unused drive slot

On the front of each unused *drive bay* (the space the drive goes into), the *slot*, is covered by a small piece of plastic. Remove the screws that attach the cover to the system unit.

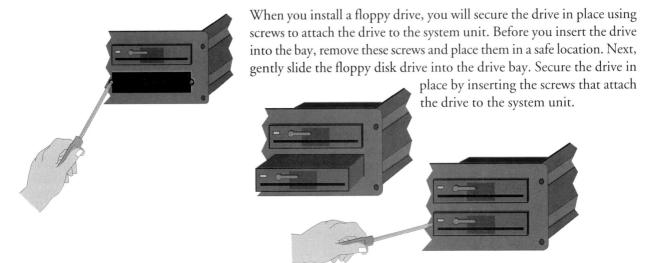

When you install a floppy drive, you will secure the drive in place using screws to attach the drive to the system unit. Before you insert the drive into the bay, remove these screws and place them in a safe location. Next, gently slide the floppy disk drive into the drive bay. Secure the drive in place by inserting the screws that attach the drive to the system unit.

For the computer to access the floppy drive, the drive must be connected to the disk controller, an expansion slot card that contains the electronics that control the drive. Within your system unit you should find an unattached ribbon cable coming from the controller.

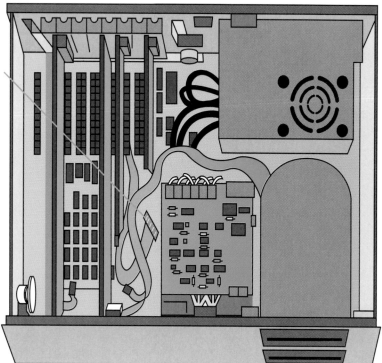

Unused ribbon cable

Align the ribbon cable to the drive connector and gently slide the cable into place. If you are connecting a 5 1/4-inch floppy, the drive will normally use edge connectors. Align the cable so that the split in the cable aligns with the connector's notch. If you are installing a 3 1/2-inch drive, the drive might use a pin connector. In this case, align the connector so that the cable's pin 1 matches the socket's pin 1. Remember, most cables indicate pin 1 by using a distinctive wire color.

Pin connector

Edge connector

Next, you must provide power to the floppy drive by connecting a power supply cable to the drive, as discussed in Lesson 22.

Replace your system unit cover and plug in and power on your PC. As your system starts, access your system's setup program as discussed in Lesson 6. You must tell your PC's CMOS memory about the floppy drive type before you can use the drive. After you specify the drive type, exit the setup program. When your system has started, the drive should be fully accessible.

INSTALLING A FLOPPY DISK DRIVE

To install a floppy disk drive, perform these steps:

1. Power off and unplug your PC system unit.

2. Remove your system unit cover, as discussed in Lesson 2.

3. Remove the small plastic cover that protects the drive slot. Remove the screws that will connect the drive to the system unit. Place the screws in a safe place.

4. Gently slide the drive into the drive bay. Secure the drive in place using the screws you just removed from the system unit.

5. Attach the drive controller ribbon cable to the drive.

6. Plug the drive into the power supply.

7. Replace and secure the system unit cover.

8. Plug in and power on your PC system unit. As your system starts, access the setup program and notify the CMOS about the new drive.

POSSIBLE INSTALLATION CHALLENGES

In most cases, installing a floppy disk drive is relatively simple. Sometimes, however, things can get more challenging. If you encounter one of the following scenarios, you might find it simpler to have a computer serviceperson perform the installation for you.

NO DRIVE RAILS

Normally, you insert the floppy disk drive into the drive bay by sliding the disk along drive rails. If your PC does not have rails for the floppy, you will need to buy and install the rails. Your challenge may become finding rails that fit both your PC and the floppy you plan to install.

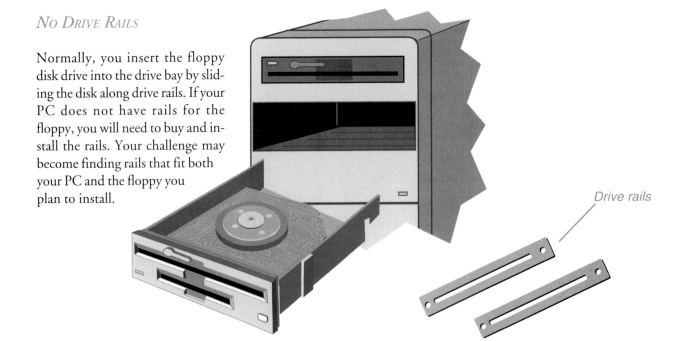

Drive rails

WRONG RIBBON CABLE CONNECTORS

As you have learned, 5 1/4- and 3 1/2-inch floppy drives sometimes use different ribbon cables. If your ribbon cable does not have the connection type you need, you will have to purchase a new cable. Before you buy a new cable, however, you will need to ensure that the cable you need is compatible with your disk controller—the electronics that operate the drive.

WRONG BIOS TYPE

In Lesson 11, you learned that the PC BIOS is a pair of chips that oversee input and output operations. Depending on the type of floppy drive you are installing, there may be times when you first need to upgrade your BIOS. When you shop for drives, determine the drive's BIOS requirements. Using the MSD command, as discussed in Lesson 36, you can display your current BIOS type. To eliminate BIOS incompatibility, some floppy drives come with their own built-in BIOS.

REVERSING DRIVES A AND B

If your system has two floppy drives, there may be times when you will want to change which drive is A and which is B. The easiest way to make this switch is simply to flip-flop the ribbon cable connectors on the floppy drives within your system unit. If your drives use different connector types, preventing the cable swap, you can buy a new cable that contains the correct connectors. After you complete the switch, you will need to notify your PC's CMOS using the setup program previously discussed.

USING A DUAL-FLOPPY DRIVE

If you install a CD-ROM or tape drive, you may find that drive bays are prime real estate. To free up a drive bay, many users are installing dual-floppy drives that combine a 5 1/4- and a 3 1/2-inch floppy into the same drive.

The steps you must perform to install the dual-floppy drive are identical to those just discussed. In most cases, the dual-floppy drive uses only one ribbon cable connector. Attach the drive A cable connector to the floppy. After you configure CMOS setup, the drive itself will correctly determine when you want to access drive A or B.

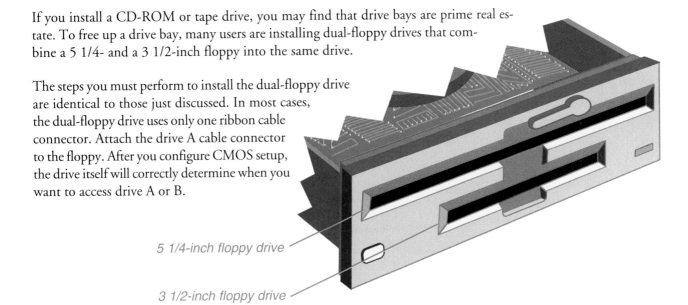

5 1/4-inch floppy drive

3 1/2-inch floppy drive

WHAT YOU NEED TO KNOW

If your PC came with only one type of floppy drive and you've always wanted to use the other type, you learned in this lesson how to remedy the situation.

Many hard disks, CD-ROM drives, and tape drives now connect to a special adapter card called a SCSI (pronounced "scuzzy") adapter or SCSI controller. In Lesson 15 you will examine the steps you need to perform to install a SCSI adapter and then how you later connect devices to create a SCSI device chain. Before you continue with Lesson 15, however, make sure that you have learned the following key concepts:

✓ If your system only has a 5 1/4- or 3 1/2-inch floppy drive, you can easily install a new floppy.

✓ When you shop for floppy drives, make sure the drive is compatible with your system BIOS.

✓ If your system does not have available drive bays, you might want to consider a dual floppy, which combines a 5 1/4- and 3 1/2-inch drive into the same unit.

✓ To exchange drives A and B, exchange the ribbon-cable connectors that attach the floppy drive to a disk controller. When you restart, you will need to inform your CMOS memory of the new setup.

Lesson 15

Installing a SCSI Adapter

SCSI (pronounced "scuzzy") is an acronym for *small computer systems interface*. A SCSI adapter is a hardware board that lets you connect up to seven high-speed devices, such as disks, CD-ROM drives, or tape drives, to your computer. With the growing need for PCs to use such devices, the SCSI adapter is becoming a key PC component. This lesson examines the steps you must perform to work with SCSI devices. By the time you finish this lesson, you will understand the following key concepts:

- How you attach devices to a SCSI adapter

- How to install a SCSI adapter

- Why you must terminate the SCSI device chain

- Why each device requires a unique SCSI address

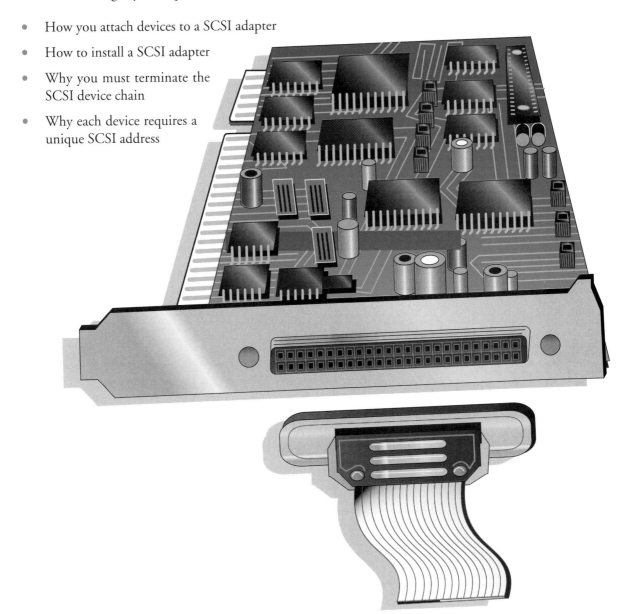

UNDERSTANDING THE SMALL COMPUTER SYSTEMS (SCSI) INTERFACE

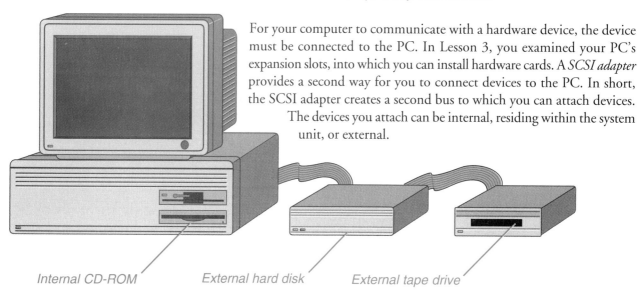

For your computer to communicate with a hardware device, the device must be connected to the PC. In Lesson 3, you examined your PC's expansion slots, into which you can install hardware cards. A *SCSI adapter* provides a second way for you to connect devices to the PC. In short, the SCSI adapter creates a second bus to which you can attach devices. The devices you attach can be internal, residing within the system unit, or external.

Internal CD-ROM   External hard disk   External tape drive

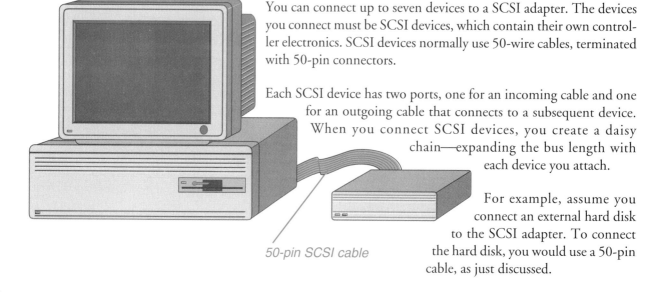

You can connect up to seven devices to a SCSI adapter. The devices you connect must be SCSI devices, which contain their own controller electronics. SCSI devices normally use 50-wire cables, terminated with 50-pin connectors.

Each SCSI device has two ports, one for an incoming cable and one for an outgoing cable that connects to a subsequent device. When you connect SCSI devices, you create a daisy chain—expanding the bus length with each device you attach.

For example, assume you connect an external hard disk to the SCSI adapter. To connect the hard disk, you would use a 50-pin cable, as just discussed.

50-pin SCSI cable

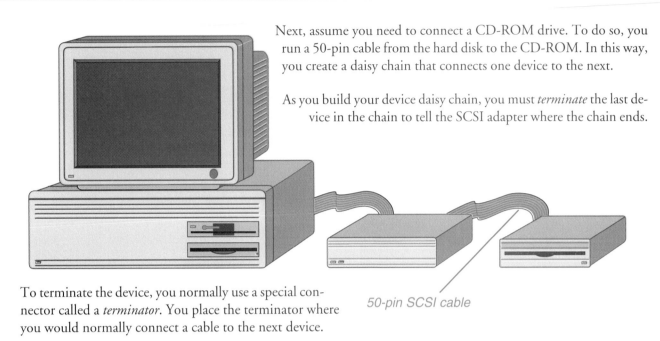

Next, assume you need to connect a CD-ROM drive. To do so, you run a 50-pin cable from the hard disk to the CD-ROM. In this way, you create a daisy chain that connects one device to the next.

As you build your device daisy chain, you must *terminate* the last device in the chain to tell the SCSI adapter where the chain ends.

50-pin SCSI cable

To terminate the device, you normally use a special connector called a *terminator*. You place the terminator where you would normally connect a cable to the next device.

Note: Some devices let you terminate devices with jumpers or even DIP switches. Refer to the documentation that accompanied your device for more specifics.

SCSI terminator

SCSI IN   SCSI OUT

SCSI DEVICES REQUIRE POWER

The 50-pin SCSI cable transmits the signals used to control or communicate with a SCSI device. In addition to connecting the SCSI cable to the device, you must also provide power to the device. In the case of an internal device, you will use one of the power supply cables, as discussed in Lesson 22. For external devices, you must plug the device into a power outlet.

UNDERSTANDING SCSI

SCSI is an acronym for *small computer system interface*. You pronounce SCSI as "scuzzy." A SCSI adapter is a hardware card that lets you connect up to seven SCSI devices. When you connect SCSI devices, you run separate SCSI cables from one device to the next, creating a daisy chain. To indicate the end of this chain, you terminate the last device by placing a special terminator in the cable port.

UNDERSTANDING SCSI DEVICE NUMBERS

When you connect devices to the SCSI adapter, the adapter must have a way to distinguish one device from the next. Thus, you must assign each device a number (called a *SCSI address*) that ranges from 0 through 7. Normally, the SCSI adapter uses device number 7. Because multiple devices are connected to the SCSI adapter, there may be times when two or more devices require the adapter's attention at the same time. In most cases, you will have one or more devices, such as a disk drive, for which a fast response is critical (if a scanner has to wait an instant, for example, the system performance won't suffer).

The SCSI adapter number lets you specify device priorities. The higher the SCSI address (such as 6 or 7), the higher the device priority. Normally, you set a device's SCSI address using DIP switches or jumpers.

INSTALLING A SCSI ADAPTER

When you install a SCSI adapter, you need to specify a DMA channel, IRQ, and port address, as discussed in Lesson 8. The documentation that accompanies your adapter should specify the board's default settings. Use the MSD command as discussed in Lesson 36 to ensure that the default settings are OK. If a conflict exists, you can change the card's settings with jumpers or DIP switches.

Next, power off and unplug your system unit. Remove the system unit cover as discussed in Lesson 2, and discharge all static from your body. Select the expansion slot into which you will install the adapter. Remove the small metal slot cover and gently insert the adapter card. Replace the screw to hold the adapter securely in place.

If you are using one or more internal SCSI devices, cable and terminate the devices. Replace and secure the system unit cover. If you are using external SCSI devices, cable and terminate the last device in the chain. Plug in and power on your PC.

Depending on your adapter or the devices you are attaching, you might need to install device-driver software. In such cases, follow the instructions specified in the manual that accompanied your device. Lesson 28 discusses device drivers in detail.

INSTALLING A SCSI ADAPTER

To install a SCSI adapter card, perform these steps:

1. Use the MSD command to determine if the card's default settings are OK. If necessary, use jumpers or DIP switches to change the board's settings so there are no conflicts.

2. Power off and unplug your PC system unit.

3. Remove your system unit cover, as discussed in Lesson 2, and discharge any static from your body.

4. Remove the expansion slot cover and gently insert the SCSI adapter card.

5. Use DIP switches or jumpers to assign the desired SCSI address to each device.

6. If you are installing internal devices, cable the devices and terminate the last one. If you are installing external devices, replace the system unit cover and then cable and terminate the devices.

WHAT YOU NEED TO KNOW

Regardless of how users work with their computers, users have one thing in common—no matter how much hard disk space they have, they find a way to consume it. In Lesson 16 you will learn how to install a hard disk. Before you continue with Lesson 15, however, make sure that you understand the following key concepts:

✓ A SCSI (pronounced "scuzzy") adapter provides a way for you to connect internal and external SCSI devices. You connect one device to the adapter and subsequent devices to one another to create a SCSI device chain.

✓ You can connect up to seven devices to a SCSI adapter. You must terminate the last device in the chain, normally using a special SCSI terminator.

✓ SCSI devices normally use a 50-pin cable.

✓ Each device in the SCSI chain must have a unique SCSI address-from 0 through 7. The higher the SCSI address, the higher the device priority.

Lesson 16

Installing a New Hard Drive

No matter how users use their computers, they normally have a similar problem—too little disk space. As programs become more complex, their storage requirements also increase. As you will read in Lesson 32, a first step you can take to combat insufficient disk space is to compress your disk using a program such as STACKER or DBLSPACE. When your compressed disk runs out of space, your next resort is to add or upgrade a new hard drive.

Hard drives are mechanical devices with moving parts. Not only do the moving parts slow down the drives, they can also fail. When a hard disk fails, you will need to replace the drive. This lesson examines the steps you must perform to install a new hard drive. By the time you finish this lesson, you will understand the following key concepts:

- How to estimate your disk storage requirements

- The difference between IDE, ESDI, and SCSI drives

- What to look for when shopping for a drive

- The steps you must perform to install an internal or external hard drive

- The software steps you must perform to access a drive

- The steps you must perform to install and use a cartridge-based drive such as a Syquest or Bernoulli drive

Your first hard disk installation can be challenging. Ideally, you should perform the upgrade with the assistance of an experienced user. Most cities have PC user's groups with members who would be very happy to assist you.

DETERMINING YOUR DISK STORAGE REQUIREMENTS

In the past, users adding a new hard disk multiplied their disk capacity by 2 to 2.5 to determine their new storage requirements. In the past, hard disk drives were also much more expensive than they are today. As a rule, most user's disk requirements grow by a factor of 3. That means that if you currently use a 100Mb drive, next year you will very likely need a 300 Mb drive.

One way to guess your future disk requirements is to multiply your current disk storage requirements by a growth factor of 3 or higher. Estimate your current requirements by adding your current disk usage to disk requirements of programs you plan to purchase over the next six months:

> New disk space = factor × (current disk space + new programs)

To start, make a list of the programs you plan to add to your disk. If you don't know a program's disk requirements, you can get a fairly close estimate from members of a local user's group.

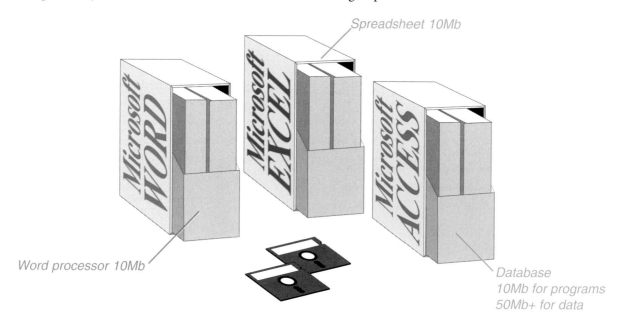

Spreadsheet 10Mb

Word processor 10Mb

Database
10Mb for programs
50Mb+ for data

In this case, assuming you plan to add these software programs and you currently use 100Mb of disk space, your future storage requirements would become the following:

> New disk space = 3 × (100 + 10 + 10 + 10 + 50)
> = 3 X (180)
> = 540Mb

As a rule, don't save a few dollars by buying a smaller drive. Most users have the ability to fill any hard drive, regardless of the disk's size.

Understanding Disk Drive Types

As you shop for hard disks, you will encounter drives labeled as ESDI, IDE, or SCSI. In short, these drive labels describe how the disk drive is attached to your computer.

ESDI is an abbreviation for Enhanced Small Device Interface. An ESDI drive normally connects to a drive controller card that you install into an expansion slot. IDE is an abbreviation for Integrated Drive Electronics. An IDE drive does not require an expansion slot card. Instead, the drive controller is built into the drive itself. In many cases, you connect an IDE drive directly to your system's motherboard. A SCSI (Small Computer Systems Interface) drive connects to a SCSI adapter card, as discussed in Lesson 15.

Before you purchase a hard drive, you need to ensure that your system will support the drive. For example, if you purchase an ESDI drive, you need to ensure that the drive will be compatible with your existing drive controller. Likewise, if you purchase an IDE drive, your computer's motherboard must support an IDE drive connection or you will need an IDE card. Finally, if you purchase a SCSI drive, you will need to have a SCSI adapter.

What to Look for in a New Drive

As you shop for hard drives, you need to know the drive's *access time*. In short, the drive's access time specifies the average time it takes for the information requested from the disk to arrive within the computer's memory. The smaller a disk's access time, the faster your disk, and hence the better your system performance. Access time is usually measured in milliseconds (ms).

Because a disk is a mechanical device, it will eventually fail. In addition to the disk's access time, you might want to examine the disk's mean time between failure (MTBF), a measurement supplied by the manufacturer that can give you a guideline about how long your disk should continue to work before a failure occurs.

Installing a New Hard Drive

Hard drives can be internal (residing within a drive bay in the PC system unit) or external. Depending on your drive type, the steps you must perform to install the drive will differ.

Installing an Internal Hard Drive

To install an internal hard drive, power off and unplug your PC. Next, remove your system unit cover as discussed in Lesson 2, and ground yourself to remove any residual static electricity from your body. If you are replacing a hard drive, first remove the ribbon cable that connects your drive to the controller. Next, remove the power plug that connects the drive to the power supply. Unscrew the drive from the drive bay, placing the screws in a safe location.

Examine your new drive's case. Some drives have a small metal label that specifies a drive type number, such as type 30. If your drive contains such a label, write down the drive type number and any other information such as the number of heads, cylinders, sectors, and so on. You will use this information later when you update your computer's CMOS after your drive installation is complete.

If you are installing a new drive, remove the plastic cover from the desired drive bay and the drive bay screws. Place the screws in a safe location. If the drive bay contains drive rails, slide your new drive into place, securing the drive with the drive bay screws.

Note: If your drive bay does not contain drive rails, you can purchase the rails from your computer retailer. However, you might find it easier to let your retailer complete the drive installation for you.

After the drive is secure within the drive bay, connect a power supply cable to the drive.

Next, use the drive's ribbon cable to connect the drive to the controller, motherboard, or to a SCSI adapter, depending on your drive type.

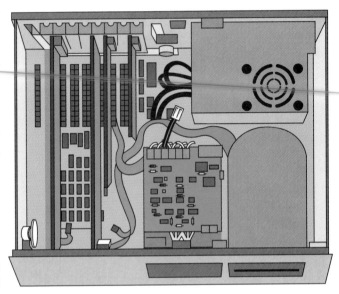

If you are installing a SCSI drive, make sure you correctly terminate the SCSI daisy chain, as discussed in Lesson 15. Replace your system unit cover and plug in your PC.

INSTALLING AN EXTERNAL HARD DRIVE

External hard drives connect to a SCSI adapter or to a proprietary card. If you need to install a special disk controller card, power off and unplug your PC.

Install the card as discussed in Lesson 5. Likewise, if you need to install a SCSI adapter, follow the steps discussed in Lesson 15. Next, attach the drive's ribbon cable to the adapter card and plug in the drive's power connector.

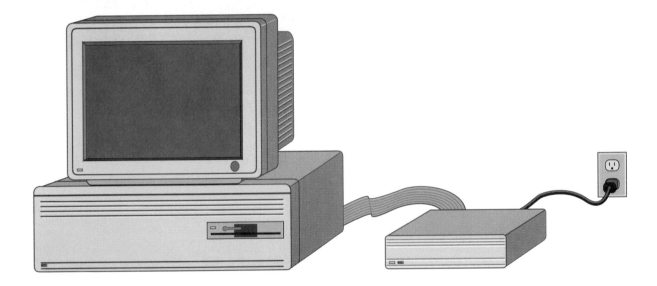

TELLING YOUR CMOS ABOUT THE DRIVE

Before your computer can access your new drive, you must assign your new drive's settings to the computer's CMOS memory. Follow the steps discussed in Lesson 6 to update the settings. Use the setting values you previously found on the drive's casing or within the documentation that accompanied your drive.

Note: Keep your drive's CMOS settings in a safe location. Should you ever need to replace your CMOS battery, the drive's many settings are often impossible to remember. If, when you update your CMOS settings, you can't locate your drive setting values, you should be able to get the setting values from the manufacturer's technical support or the service division at your computer retailer. Also, several books contain listings of the settings for virtually every drive known.

PREPARING YOUR NEW DISK FOR USE BY DOS

Before DOS can store information on your new disk, you must first partition and then format your disk. To partition your disk, you use the DOS FDISK command. To format your disk, you use the FORMAT command.

If you are adding a second hard drive, your existing hard drive should contain the FDISK and FORMAT commands. If you don't have an existing hard drive (you are replacing your previous drive), you must work from a floppy disk that contains the commands.

To work from a floppy, you will need to boot (start) your system using a bootable floppy disk. Next, you need to ensure that the floppy disk contains the FDISK and FORMAT commands. For information on FDISK and FORMAT, turn to the book *Rescued by DOS*, Jamsa Press, 1993.

PARTITIONING YOUR DISK

Before you can use a hard disk, it must be formatted; before DOS can recognize a disk to format, the disk must be *partitioned* into one or more logical collections called *partitions*. This is often done by the manufacturer or retailer of the drive before you buy it. If not, you use the DOS FDISK command. (Before you partition a drive, you must first inform the CMOS about the disk and its type.)

Drive C 100Mb

Drive D 100Mb

Drive E 100Mb

FDISK divides a disk into at least one partition, each having a minimum size of 1Mb, with the total of all partitions equaling no more than the entire capacity of the disk. Each partition is viewed by DOS as a logical disk drive and gets its own drive letter. For example, if you have a 300Mb drive, you might prefer that DOS think of the drive as three 100Mb drives named C, D, and E.

Users often divide a hard disk into multiple drives to organize their files better. For example, they might store programs on drive C, files for work on drive D, and files for school on drive E. When you use multiple drives in this way, a command you execute for drive D, (such as the delete command), will not affect files on a different drive. In this way, users have an additional level of file protection.

Users who have different operating systems (for example UNIX, DR DOS, or OS/2) on the same drive have one partition for each operating system, so that they can start up in the system they need.

To change how DOS views the drive (one drive or several), you use the FDISK command. To begin, you invoke FDISK from the DOS prompt:

A:\> FDISK   <ENTER>

FDISK will display a menu of options similar to that shown in Figure 16.1.

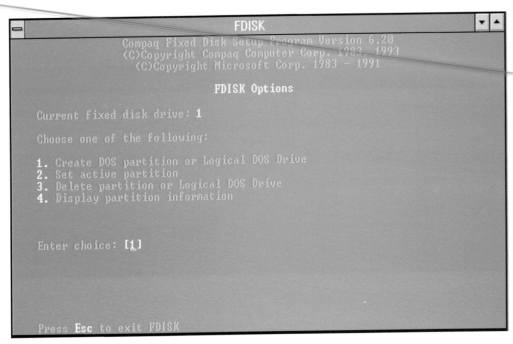

Figure 16.1 *The FDISK main menu.*

For the detailed steps you must perform from the FDISK menu, turn to the DOS documentation that accompanied your disk drive, as well as the book *Rescued by DOS*, Jamsa Press, 1993.

Note: *If you are installing a second hard drive, choose the option that lets you select the new drive before you attempt to create a partition.*

FORMATTING YOUR DISK PARTITIONS

After you use FDISK to partition your hard disk, you need to format each disk partition. To format your disk, you use the DOS FORMAT command. If you have a working hard drive (you are adding a second drive), your existing drive should contain the FORMAT command. If you are replacing your hard drive, you will need to work with a floppy disk that contains FORMAT.

For your computer to start DOS, your hard disk must contain special operating system files. To place these needed files on your disk, you invoke the FORMAT command using the /S switch.

Warning! Use the FORMAT command with great care. If you inadvertently format the wrong drive, the information the drive contained will be lost! If you are not sure how to format the correct drive, have an experienced user assist you.

FORMATTING A SECOND HARD DRIVE

If you are installing a second disk and you have partitioned the second hard drive, you can format that drive using the FORMAT command contained on your existing hard drive (drive C). Assuming that your new hard drive is drive D (the FDISK command will determine the drive letter), you would format the drive as follows:

If your new disk drive uses a different drive letter, simply substitute your disk drive letter for drive D in the command just shown.

FORMATTING A DRIVE FROM A FLOPPY

If you have replaced your computer's only hard drive, you will need to format your drive from a floppy disk. To begin, the floppy disk must be bootable. In other words, the floppy must contain the files that DOS needs to start. Next, the floppy must also contain the FORMAT command.

*Note: If you intend to replace your only hard drive, make sure you have a **dependable** boot floppy disk that has the FORMAT command on it **before** you remove the old drive.*

To format your hard disk so DOS can start from it, use the following command:

FORMATTING EACH DRIVE PARTITION

As you have learned, using the FDISK command, you can divide a single hard disk into multiple drives called partitions. For example, you might divide a 200Mb hard disk into two 100Mb drives named C and D. After you partition the drives, you must format each drive.

INSTALLING A HARD DISK DRIVE

Depending on whether you are installing an internal hard drive or external drive, the steps you must perform will differ slightly.

Internal Drive

To install an internal drive:

1. Power off and unplug your system unit and remove the system unit cover.

2. Secure the drive into a drive bay slot.

3. Connect the drive's ribbon cable to the drive controller.

4. Plug the drive into the power supply.

5. Replace and secure the system unit cover.

External Drive

To install an external drive:

1. Power off and unplug your system unit.

2. If necessary, install a hard drive adapter card within the system unit.

3. Connect the drive's ribbon cable to the adapter card.

4. Plug in the drive's power cable.

Software Operations

After you have installed the drive, closed up the system unit, and powered up and started the computer, you need to do the following:

1. Update your computer's CMOS settings.

2. Use the FDISK command to partition the drive.

3. Use the FORMAT command to format the disk drive.

INSTALLING A CARTRIDGE-BASED DRIVE

When the size of the files you must exchange with other users exceeds the capacity of a floppy disk by enough to make use of the MSBACKUP unfeasible, you have two choices. First you can place the files onto a tape drive, as discussed in Lesson 24. Second, you can place the files on to a *disk cartridge*. A disk cartridge is a cross between a floppy and hard disk. Like a floppy, the cartridge is removable. Like a hard disk, the cartridge can store large amounts of information (over 80Mb of information depending on the drive and cartridge type).

Disk cartridge drives can be internal or external devices. Most cartridge-based systems are SCSI based. Some, however, use a special controller card. To install a cartridge device, follow the steps discussed in this lesson for internal or external drives.

After the cartridge drive is in place, you will need to install special device driver software. The device driver software will determine the drive letter you will use to access the drive (such as drive E or F). You do not use the FDISK command with a cartridge drive.

Note: If the highest drive letter you use is beyond E, don't forget to update the LASTDRIVE= setting in your CONFIG.SYS to accommodate the highest drive letter you will use.

Before you can store information on a cartridge, you must format each cartridge using the DOS FORMAT command, just as you would format a floppy disk. After the cartridge is formatted, you can treat it like a large floppy—inserting and removing the cartridge as your needs require.

Note: If you need to exchange files with a Mac user, you can purchase software that lets you read or write files to a cartridge disk in Mac format. Likewise, the Mac user can purchase software that lets Mac read or write PC (DOS) files.

WHAT YOU NEED TO KNOW

In Lesson 17, you will learn how to install and use a modem and fax/modem to connect your PC to the world. Before you continue with Lesson 17, make sure that you understand the following key concepts:

✓ Before you purchase a hard disk, you need to estimate your disk storage requirements. To estimate your new requirements, multiply your current disk requirements by a factor of 3.

✓ As you shop for a disk, you will encounter the terms ESDI, IDE, and SCSI. In short, these terms describe how you connect the drive to your computer.

✓ After you install your hard disk, you must update your computer's CMOS settings.

✓ Before you can use a newly installed drive, you must first use the DOS FDISK command to partition the drive and then you must format each disk partition.

✓ If you have never used the FDISK or FORMAT commands in the past, have an experienced user assist you. An inadvertent error with either of these commands can quickly destroy all the information a second disk contains.

✓ If you need to exchange very large files with another user, you can place the files on to a magnetic tape or you can use a disk cartridge. A disk cartridge is best viewed as a cross between a floppy disk and a hard disk.

Lesson 17

Installing a Modem

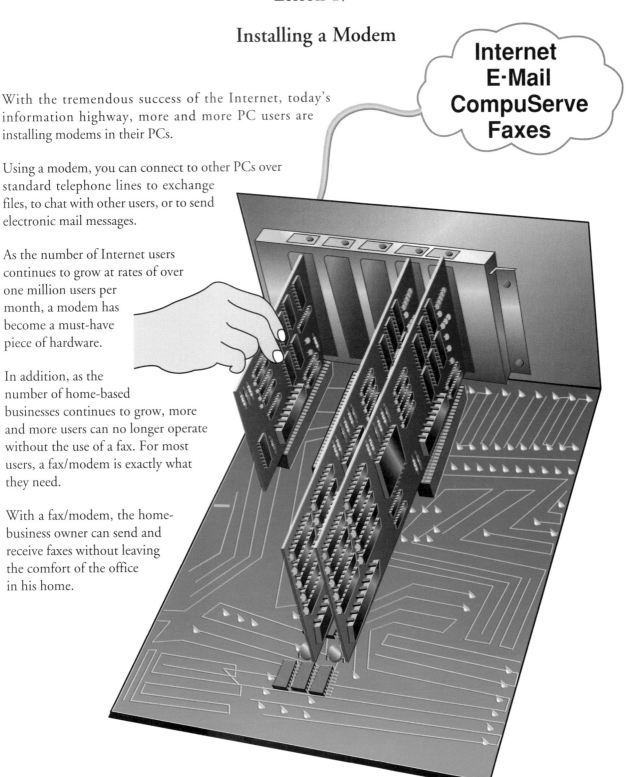

**Internet
E-Mail
CompuServe
Faxes**

With the tremendous success of the Internet, today's information highway, more and more PC users are installing modems in their PCs.

Using a modem, you can connect to other PCs over standard telephone lines to exchange files, to chat with other users, or to send electronic mail messages.

As the number of Internet users continues to grow at rates of over one million users per month, a modem has become a must-have piece of hardware.

In addition, as the number of home-based businesses continues to grow, more and more users can no longer operate without the use of a fax. For most users, a fax/modem is exactly what they need.

With a fax/modem, the home-business owner can send and receive faxes without leaving the comfort of the office in his home.

This lesson examines the steps you must perform to install a modem. By the time you finish this lesson, you will understand the following key concepts:

- How modems work

- The difference between modem speeds

- The benefits of a fax/modem

- The steps you must perform to install a modem

- The purpose of data communications settings and how you assign them

- The purpose of fax and modem software

At first glance, you might think that installing a modem is a very easy task. Unfortunately, default modem settings often conflict with your existing hardware devices. As a result, your modem may hang up when you move your mouse or your mouse itself may stop working. If you follow the steps presented in this lesson, however, you will reduce the possibility of such conflicts.

How Modems Work

A *modem* is a hardware device that lets you connect two computers using standard phone lines. First the sending computer's modem *mo*dulates the computer's digital signals into analog signals that can pass over the phone lines. Then the receiving computer's modem *dem*odulates the analog signal back into the digital signal that the computers understand.

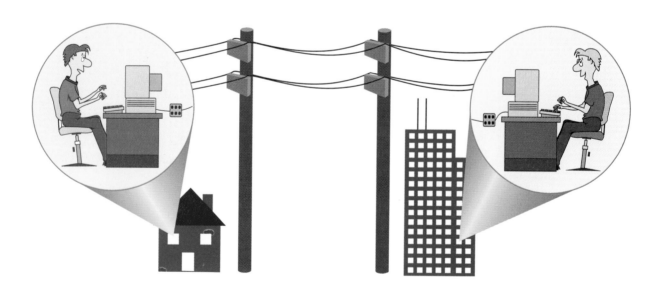

Using the modem, your computer essentially calls the second computer, which in turn, answers the incoming call. The two computers can reside across town, across the country, or even around the world. The cost to call a second computer outside of your city is identical to making a long distance phone call.

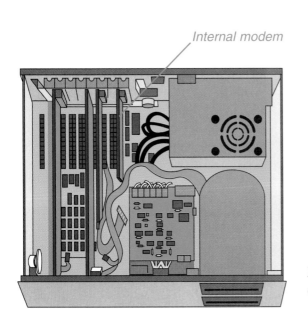

Internal modem

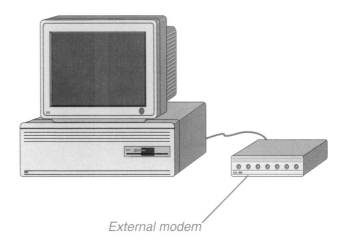

External modem

Modems can be internal (residing within your system unit) or external. In either case, the modem's purpose is identical.

UNDERSTANDING MODEMS

A modem is a hardware device that lets two computers communicate over standard phone lines. When you use a modem, one computer calls a second computer, much as you would make a long distance phone call. Using modems, you can exchange files or chat with other users or you can send electronic mail. A fax/modem is a modem that also has the ability to send information to a remote fax machine.

UNDERSTANDING MODEM SPEEDS

When two modems communicate, they must first agree on a communication speed. As you shop for modems, you will encounter speeds such as 2400, 9600, and 14400 (called 14.4K). If you have an older modem, its speed may be 300 or 1200. Modem speed is expressed in terms of baud rate. In general, baud stands for bits per second.

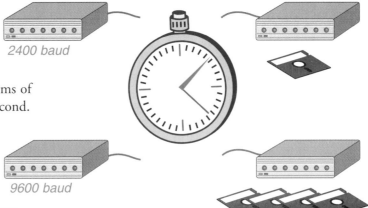

2400 baud

9600 baud

As you know, computers work in terms of 1s and 0s—bits (binary digits). The same is true for modems. A 2400 baud modem, for example, can send or receive 2400 bits of information in a second. Likewise, a 9600 baud modem can send or receive 9600 bits per second. As you can see, the 9600 baud modem is four times faster than its 2400 baud counterpart, which can save you a lot on phone bills.

MODEM UPGRADES ARE A SMART INVESTMENT

If you are using an older modem whose speed is less than 9600 baud, you should consider an immediate modem upgrade. Like all PC hardware, the price of modems has come down drastically over the last year. You can now buy a very fast 14.4K baud (14,400 bits per second) modem for less than $200. With the rapid growth of the information highway, your modem use is likely to increase. The faster your modem, the less time you will waste waiting for your modem to send or receive information. When you purchase a new modem, make sure you purchase a fax/modem discussed later in this lesson.

When you send files from one computer to another, keep in mind that file sizes are expressed in terms of bytes (eight bits) and not bits. To send a 64Kb (65,536 bytes) file, for example, means you need to send over 524,288 bits (65,536 × 8). Table 17.1 lists the approximate amount of time the file transfer would require at different modem speeds.

Modem Speed	File Size	Transfer Times
300 baud	64Kb	Over 29 minutes
1200 baud	64Kb	Over 7 minutes
2400 baud	64Kb	Over 3 minutes
9600 baud	64Kb	About 1 minute
14.4K baud	64Kb	About 30 seconds

Table 17.1 Transfer times for a 64Kb file at different baud rates.

Note: Consider phone charges for the above times, and you will see why buying a fast modem is a good idea, however, modem communication takes two computers—it can only be as fast as the slower modem, no matter how fast the faster is.

UNDERSTANDING MODEM SPEEDS

Modem speeds are expressed in terms of baud rate (bits per second). The higher the baud rate, the faster the modem. Typical baud rates include 2400, 9600, 14.4K (14400), 28.8K (28800) baud. If you are not currently using a 14.4K or faster baud modem, you should consider a modem upgrade.

BENEFITS OF A FAX/MODEM

A fax/modem is simply a modem that can also send and receive faxes. Most newer modems are fax/modems.

Using a fax/modem, you can connect to both fax machines and other computers.

Fax/Modem

Phone Lines

Modem

Fax

Fax/modems are ideal for travelers who carry a laptop PC with them. When you receive a fax using a fax/modem, you can view the fax on your screen or you can print it on your printer.

To send a fax, however, the document must be electronic; in other words, it must be stored on your disk. You **Fax/Modem** cannot send a paper fax using a fax/modem. If you have a scanner, you can scan the paper image into your computer as an electronic image; then you can send that image. Many fax programs let you "print" to the fax/modem directly from the current application (such as a word processor, draw program, or spreadsheet).

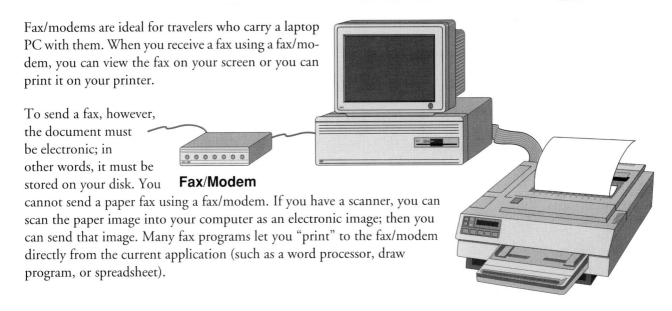

INSTALLING YOUR MODEM

As you have learned, a modem can be internal, residing within your system unit. This section examines the steps you must perform to install both modem types.

INSTALLING AN INTERNAL MODEM

When you install a modem, you need to identify which interrupt request line (IRQ) the modem will use to signal the computer and the serial port (such as COM1 or COM2), the modem will use. As discussed in Lesson 8, the modem must use a unique IRQ number. Likewise, when you select a serial port, you must select a port that is not in use. To determine the available IRQ settings, use the MSD command, discussed in Lesson 36. MSD will display the current IRQ settings, as shown in Figure 17.1.

```
 File  Utilities  Help
┌─────────────────────────── IRQ Status ───────────────────────────┐
│  IRQ   Address    Description        Detected          Handled By  │
│  ───   ────────   ───────────        ──────────        ──────────  │
│   0    1BDB:03F8  Timer Click        Yes               DOSCAP.COM   │
│   1    1BDB:0417  Keyboard           Yes               DOSCAP.COM   │
│   2    0467:0057  Second 8259A       Yes               Default Handlers │
│   3    0467:006F  COM2: COM4:        COM2:             Default Handlers │
│   4    1AAF:0095  COM1: COM3:        COM1: Serial Mouse DOSCAP.COM  │
│   5    0467:009F  LPT2:              No                Default Handlers │
│   6    0467:00B7  Floppy Disk        Yes               Default Handlers │
│   7    0070:06F4  LPT1:              Yes               System Area  │
│   8    0467:0052  Real-Time Clock    Yes               Default Handlers │
│   9    F000:EED2  Redirected IRQ2    Yes               BIOS         │
│  10    0467:00CF  (Reserved)                           Default Handlers │
│  11    0467:00E7  (Reserved)                           Default Handlers │
│  12    0467:00FF  (Reserved)                           Default Handlers │
│  13    F000:EEDB  Math Coprocessor   Yes               BIOS         │
│  14    0467:0117  Fixed Disk         Yes               Default Handlers │
│  15    F000:914A  (Reserved)                           BIOS         │
│                                                                    │
│                        ▐ OK ▌                                       │
└────────────────────────────────────────────────────────────────────┘
 IRQ Status: Displays current usage of hardware interrupts.
```

Figure 17.1 Displaying IRQ settings with MSD.

In the previous example, you would need to select IRQ 10, 11, 12, or 15. Once you determine the correct setting, you can use a jumper or DIP switch to select the IRQ setting on the board.

To select the modem's serial port setting, you must determine which serial ports are currently in use. If you are not using a serial printer, then you normally only have to worry about a serial mouse.

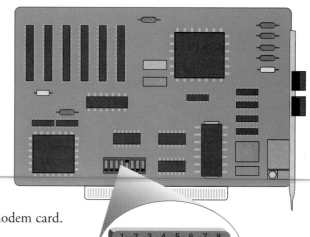

If your mouse uses COM1, for example, you would assign your modem to COM2. To select the modem serial port, you normally use a jumper or DIP switch on the modem card.

The PC can support up to four serial ports, COM1 through COM4. Unfortunately, in most cases, you can only use two serial devices at any given time. As it turns out, COM1 and COM3 share a key address, as do COM2 and COM4. If you attach your mouse to COM1 and your modem to COM3, a conflict will occur due to this shared address.

After you determine the correct IRQ and serial port, power off and unplug your system unit. Next, remove your system unit cover, as discussed in Lesson 2, and rid yourself of any static charge. Locate an unused expansion slot and gently insert the modem card. Secure the card in place and replace the system unit cover.

If you examine the back of the PC system unit, you will find modem ports for phone lines.

Connect a phone cable from your phone wall outlet to the modem port labeled **Line**.

Next, if you like, connect your phone to the port that is labeled **Phone**.

Connecting your phone to the modem is optional; the modem will work perfectly well without a phone attached to it. Plug in and power on your PC system unit.

INSTALLING AN INTERNAL MODEM

To install an internal modem, perform the following steps:

1. Determine the IRQ and serial port the modem will use.

2. Power off and unplug your PC system unit.

3. Remove your system unit cover, as discussed in Lesson 2, and rid yourself of static charge.

4. Gently insert the modem card into an expansion slot.

5. Replace and secure your system unit cover.

6. Connect your phone wall outlet to the modem port labeled **Line**. If you wish, connect your phone to the modem port labeled **Phone**.

7. Plug in and power on your PC system unit.

INSTALLING AN EXTERNAL MODEM

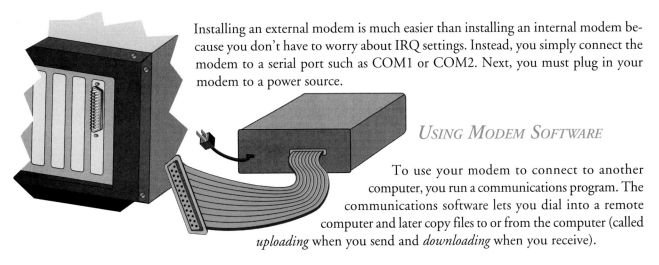

Installing an external modem is much easier than installing an internal modem because you don't have to worry about IRQ settings. Instead, you simply connect the modem to a serial port such as COM1 or COM2. Next, you must plug in your modem to a power source.

USING MODEM SOFTWARE

To use your modem to connect to another computer, you run a communications program. The communications software lets you dial into a remote computer and later copy files to or from the computer (called *uploading* when you send and *downloading* when you receive).

When you purchase a modem, you will normally receive a floppy disk that contains such software. In addition, Windows provides a built-in software communications program named Terminal, which will meet most of your needs.

UNDERSTANDING DATA COMMUNICATION SETTINGS

When two computers communicate over phone lines, the computers must agree on several settings, such as how fast they will send and receive information, how much information they will send and receive at one time, and so on.

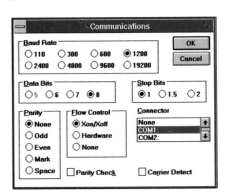

These key settings are called *data communication settings*. When connecting to a bulletin board system, for example, the person who runs the BBS will tell you the correct settings you should use. Likewise, if you are using your computer to connect to the Internet, your Internet provider will tell you the correct settings you use should use.

You assign data communication settings using your modem software. Normally, your modem software will provide a dialog box, similar to that shown in Figure 17.2, that lets you specify the data communication settings.

Figure 17.2 A communication settings dialog box.

Do not let data communication settings intimidate you. Once you know the settings you need to connect to a specific computer, you simply use a dialog box similar to the one just shown to assign the settings. After that, you can essentially ignore the settings function.

Using Fax Software

Most modems sold today are fax/modems, which means you can use the modem to send faxes to remote fax machines. To send a fax, you will need to run special fax software. Typically, such software lets you type in your fax message and then dial and connect to a remote fax machine to send the fax. Likewise, many fax software programs let you receive and print faxes while you use your computer to run other programs!

One of the most popular fax software programs is Delrina's WinFax PRO. Using WinFax, you can create your fax message using a word processor such as Microsoft Word. To send your fax, you then simply print the file to your fax/modem, just as if the fax/modem were a printer. The WinFax software will ask you to type in the phone number for the remote fax. As the software sends the fax, a dialog box appears on your screen that lets you monitor the fax progress.

What You Need to Know

The modem (especially fax/modem) is becoming one of the very important pieces of equipment that a computer user can have. Using a modem, you can deliver a document across the country (or the world!) in seconds, for the price of a long distance phone call. In this lesson you have learned how to install a modem into your system.

Over the next year, more than five million users will install multimedia sound cards within their systems. In Lesson 18 you will learn how to install a sound card. Before you continue with Lesson 18, however, make sure that you have learned the following key concepts:

- ✓ A modem is a hardware device that lets two computers communicate over telephone lines.

- ✓ When you shop for modems, you will encounter different speeds, such as 1200, 2400, 9600, or 14.4K baud. The faster a modem's speed, the faster your response time will be when you use the modem to exchange information. You can only send as fast as the other modem can receive.

- ✓ A fax/modem is a modem that lets you connect to a remote fax to send or receive faxes. When you shop for a modem, make sure you purchase a fax/modem—you will quickly find that you will send most of your faxes directly from your PC.

- ✓ To use your modem to connect to a remote computer to send or receive faxes, you must use special modem or fax/modem software. In most cases, when you purchase a modem, you will receive a floppy disk that contains the necessary software.

- ✓ Before two computers can communicate using modems, the computers must agree on different settings, such how fast they will exchange information. You can set these key settings, called data communication settings, using your communication software.

Lesson 18

Installing a Multimedia Sound Card

With the multimedia craze sweeping the nation, users are quickly adding sound boards to their PCs. In the past, very few programs could take advantage of a sound board. Today, however, that situation is changing quickly. Newer programs use sound effects, audio and video instruction, and can even play back audio CDs!

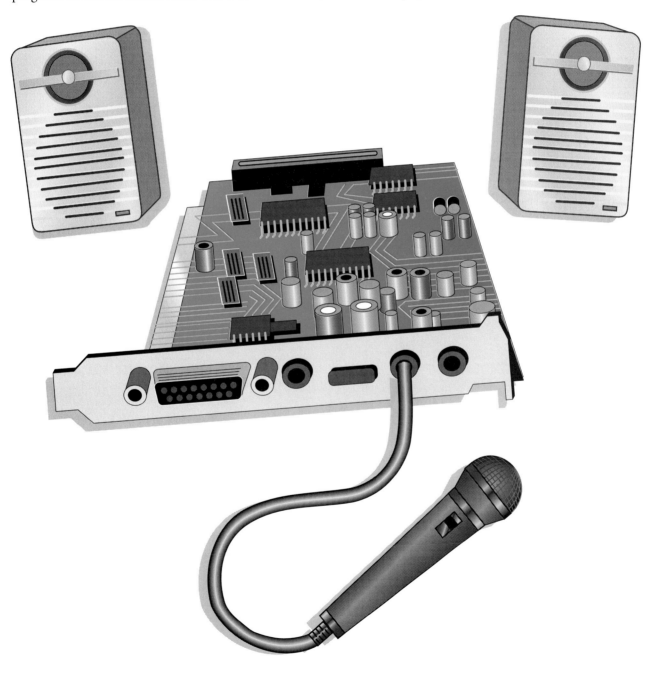

This lesson presents the steps you must perform to install a sound card. By the time you finish this lesson, you will understand the following concepts:

- The purpose of a sound card and the different capabilities you will encounter

- How you use the different sound card ports

- The steps you must perform to install a sound card

- The common conflicts you may encounter when you install a sound card

If you have not yet purchased a sound card, you need to visit your computer retailer and take one for a test drive. As the growth of multimedia programs continues to explode, a sound card is becoming a must-have device.

WHAT YOU'LL NEED

Before you get started on this lesson, make sure that you have the following readily available:

1. A PC tool kit with a screwdriver

2. A container within which you can place the chassis screws

3. A well-lit workspace with room for you to place the chassis

4. A new sound card and speakers

Although sound cards differ in price and quality, most sound cards provide the following capabilities:

- Recording via an external microphone

- Recording via a line-in source

- MIDI interface

- WAV file playback

- Audio CD-ROM playback

There are several aspects in which sound cards differ from one another. Here are some points to consider when you are looking for a sound card:

- If possible, listen to playback on computers with each card.

- There are eight-bit sound cards and 16-bit sound cards. The 16-bit cards, slightly more expensive, use more memory to describe the notes, and, thus, the sound is better. If you can, get a 16-bit card.

- Some sound cards come bundled with powered speakers (with a small amplifier built into each speaker), sometimes saving some money over a separately purchased card and speakers. With others, you must buy the speakers separately, which could be an advantage if you are plugging right into a stereo that has its own speakers.

- The CD-ROM interface of some sound cards is SCSI compatible. If SCSI compatibility is a concern, make sure that the sound card supports "true" SCSI. Ask your dealer.

- Sound cards purchased for general use should be "Sound Blaster compatible."

- Better sound quality comes from boards using "wave-table synthesis" than comes from those using "FM synthesis."

- Sound boards with a Digital Signal Processor load processing from the CPU to the DSP on the sound board, freeing up your CPU.

A sound board is simply a card you install into one of the PC's expansion slots. As you can see, a sound card has several ports.

The sections that follow discuss each port in detail.

USING THE SOUND CARD'S SPEAKER PORT

When you use a sound card, you can connect external speakers, headphones, or even (if you're a big-sound fan) a line input to your stereo to the card's speaker port. If you are using external speakers, you will plug one speaker into the sound card and the second speaker into the first. The little amplifier that drives most external speakers can be powered by battery.

In most cases, however, you will want to invest in a small power supply, which lets you plug the speakers (actually, their little amps) into a standard wall outlet.

Audio-in

Microphone port

Speaker

Midi

USING THE SOUND CARD'S MICROPHONE PORT

You can use the sound card to record voice, music, or other sounds with an external microphone. When you connect a microphone to the sound card's port, you do not need to provide the microphone with any additional power. The sound card will provide the necessary power to the microphone.

Most microphones provide an On/Off switch that you can use to control recording. In most cases, however, you will use a software program to tell the sound card when to record and when to stop.

USING THE SOUND CARD'S AUDIO LINE INPUT

In addition to using a microphone for recording, most sound cards provide a port for direct audio input. Using the audio-in port, you can record music from a stereo system or other sources, such a television or VCR. In addition, many users will plug their PC's CD-ROM directly into the audio-in port. In this way, you can use the sound card to play the same audio CDs you would play on your stereo system.

USING THE SOUND CARD'S MIDI INPUT

MIDI is an acronym for Musical Instrument Digital Interface. In short, MIDI defines the standard that allows digital electronic instruments, such as an electronic piano keyboard, to interface with a computer and its software.

Most sound cards provide a MIDI interface that looks similar to a small parallel or serial port. When you connect a MIDI device to this port, you can use the device to play back songs that have been recorded digitally. This has opened up a whole new world of recording, sequencing, and tone control for musicians and recording engineers. In addition, most sound cards let you connect a joystick device to the MIDI port for use with computer games.

INSTALLING A SOUND CARD

The steps you must perform to install a sound card are very similar to those you perform for other cards. To begin, power off and unplug your PC system unit. Next, remove the system unit cover, as discussed in Lesson 2, and discharge any static from your body. Locate an unused expansion slot and remove the slot's metal cover. Gently insert the sound card into the slot, securing the card in place with the screw you just removed from the slot cover.

Replace and secure the system unit cover. Next, connect your external speakers to the sound card's speaker port. Plug in and power on your PC and the external speakers. When your system starts, you will need to install device driver software and run other programs in order to use the card.

INSTALLING A SOUND CARD

To install a sound card, perform these steps:

1. Power off and unplug your PC system unit.

2. Remove the system unit cover, placing the screws in a safe location, and discharge any static from your body.

3. Locate an unused expansion slot and remove the slot's metal cover.

4. Gently insert the sound card into the expansion slot and secure the card in place.

5. Replace and secure the system unit cover.

6. Connect the external speakers to the sound card's speaker port.

7. Plug in and power on the PC system unit and the external speakers.

INSTALLING SOUND CARD SOFTWARE

After you install the sound card, you must install device driver software before you can put the card to use. If you plan to use the card for DOS and Windows programs, you will need to install device drivers for both. As you unpacked your sound card, you should have found one or more floppy disks that contain the device driver files. The documentation that accompanied your sound card should specify the steps you must perform to install the device driver software. Also, Lessons 28 and 29 discuss DOS and Windows device drivers.

The disks that accompanied your sound card might also include sample DOS and Windows programs that support sounds, and might even provide some sample sound files. Within Windows, the Accessories group provides the Sound Recorder program, with which you can record and playback sound files. For more information on using the Sound Recorder program, turn to the book *Rescued by Windows*, Jamsa Press, 1993.

RESOLVING COMMON CONFLICTS

If your sound card does not work or another card stops working when you use your sound card, your PC has a hardware conflict, as discussed in Lesson 8. The most common conflict is selecting a sound card interrupt request (IRQ) that is already in use. In addition, most sound cards require an I/O address as well as a DMA channel. To change a sound card's settings, you must change jumpers or DIP switches that reside on the card. If you experience problems with your sound card, follow the steps discussed in Lesson 8 to resolve the conflict.

WHAT YOU NEED TO KNOW

As interest in multimedia explodes in the PC world, a sound card is becoming a must-have item for PC users. In this lesson, you have learned what sound cards are capable of and how to install them.

As more and more users spend longer hours in front of their monitors, many users have realized how a quality monitor can reduce their eye strain. In Lesson 19 you will examine the different ways two monitors can differ. You will also examine the steps you must perform to upgrade your monitor. Before you continue with Lesson 19, however, make sure that you have learned the following key concepts:

- ✓ A sound card is a hardware board that lets your PC record and play back sounds.

- ✓ The sound card can play back sounds using external speakers or headphones. In addition, you can connect the audio-out line to a stereo amplifier or other device with line-level inputs.

- ✓ With a sound card, you can record sounds using an external microphone or an audio-in source. Using the audio-in source, you can record music from a stereo or other device with line-level outputs such as a VCR.

- ✓ Many sound cards include a MIDI interface, which allows musical instruments and recording and sequencing devices to interface with your computer and special music software.

- ✓ When you install a sound card, you can experience three types of conflicts: an IRQ, I/O address, or DMA channel conflict. To resolve these conflicts, follow the steps that are listed in Lesson 8.

- ✓ After you install a sound card you will need to install a device driver and software programs that let you use the card.

Lesson 19

Upgrading Your Monitor

As the number of hours you spend in front of the PC increases, so too does the importance of having a good monitor. In Lesson 20 you will learn about video cards which provide the first half of the picture. In this lesson you will about monitors. If you think about it for a moment, installing a monitor is very easy. You simply connect the monitor to the video adapter card and then plug in and power on the monitor. Thus, this lesson takes a look at several factors you should consider when you shop for a monitor. By the time you finish this lesson, you will understand the following key concepts:

- How monitor ergonomics make your monitor easier to use
- How a monitor displays an image
- How resolution and sharpness relate
- The difference between interlaced and non-interlaced monitors

UNDERSTANDING MONITOR ERGONOMICS

Because of the long hours users spend in front of their monitors, designers have invested tremendous efforts to make monitors more people friendly. In the past, an ergonomic monitor was one that would adjust up and down or rotate from left to right.

Today, however, some monitors let you rotate them 90 degrees, to represent the shape of your current document better.

In a similar way, older monitors let you fight glare by adjusting the monitor's brightness and contrast, much like you would adjust a TV.

Today, many monitors support glare suppressing screens that you can insert or remove as required. In addition to these mechanical improvements, newer monitors support sharper images and truer colors. The sections that follow discuss the behind-the-scenes operations that control your monitor's capabilities.

HOW A MONITOR DISPLAYS AN IMAGE

Monitors display characters and images by illuminating small dots on the screen called picture elements or *pixels*.

As it turns out, each pixel is actually made up of a red, green, and blue element. By illuminating these three elements at different intensities, the monitor is able to change the pixel's color.

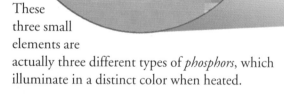

These three small elements are actually three different types of *phosphors*, which illuminate in a distinct color when heated.

To illuminate the phosphors, the monitor contains three precise electron guns (one for each phosphor color) that it can aim and fire.

To display characters or images on your screen, the monitor quickly fires the electron guns across and then down your screen.

UNDERSTANDING MONITOR FREQUENCIES

As you just learned, the monitor displays images by illuminating phosphors using three electron guns. To display an entire screen image, the monitor repeatedly scans the guns across and down

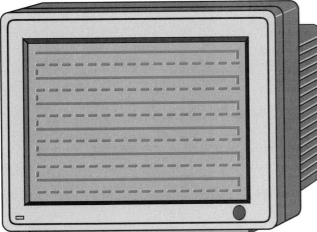

the screen. With each scan, the monitor illuminates red, green, and blue phosphors. Unfortunately, to maintain an image, the phosphors must be continually refreshed (reheated). As such, the monitor must move the electron guns very quickly. In fact, VGA monitors, for example, refresh a new line of pixels over 30,000 times a second!

The speed at which a monitor starts refreshing a new line of pixels is called the *horizontal refresh rate*. Monitors refresh lines of pixels from left to right across the screen. When the guns reach the right edge of the screen, the monitor turns the electron guns off as it aims the guns to the start of the next line.

In a similar way, the speed at which the monitor refreshes the entire screen is called the *vertical refresh rate*. Common vertical refresh rates range from 50 to 72 times per second. When the electron guns reach the bottom of the screen display, the monitor turns off the guns while it aims them back at the upper-left corner of the screen.

UNDERSTANDING HZ AND KHZ

When you express the number of times an operation is performed per second, you can use the term *hertz,* which is often abbreviated as Hz. A monitor that refreshes the screen 72 times per second is refreshing at 72Hz. If an operation is performed thousands of times per second, you can use the term *kilohertz,* which is abbreviated as KHz. A monitor that refreshes lines of pixels 15,000 times per second, for example, refreshes at 15KHz.

Monitor speeds are expressed in terms of their vertical refresh rate. Monitors support either a fixed refresh rate or multiple rates. For example, an EGA monitor supports a refresh rate of 60Hz. Likewise, a VGA monitor will support either a rate of 60 or 70Hz. *Multisynch* monitors have the ability to refresh the screen at different rates. Thus, you can typically plug a multisynch monitor into any video card. Although multisynch monitors are very flexible, they are also more expensive. If you are shopping for a fixed-rate video monitor, make sure the monitor will support your video card.

THE ADVANTAGE OF MULTISYNCH MONITORS

A multisynch monitor is a monitor that you can plug into a video card that refreshes the screen at 60, 70, or 72Hz. Thus, you can view a multisynch monitor as plug and play. If you are working with a monitor that is not multisynch, you will not have such a luxury.

UNDERSTANDING RESOLUTION AND SHARPNESS

As you have learned, the monitor displays images by illuminating pixels. *Resolution* is the measure of the number of pixels the monitor can display on your screen. Common resolutions include 640×480, 800×600, and 1024×768.

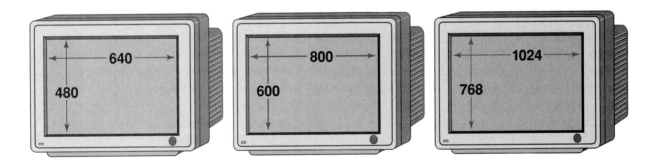

As a rule, the higher the image resolution, the sharper the image. The following illustrates how the same illustration might appear at three different resolutions.

When you shop for a monitor, it is important that you consider the monitor's resolution. Equally important, however, is the resolution your video card supports. Keeping in mind that the higher the resolution, the sharper the image, you then need to compare monitors, ideally side by side and definitely with both using the same video card and video mode (resolution and number of colors), to compare sharpness. Just because two monitors have the same resolution does not mean the monitor will have the same image *sharpness*. Other factors, such as hardware design and quality, influence monitor sharpness.

One feature often used to measure a monitor's sharpness is *dot pitch*, which describes the distance between successive phosphor colors.

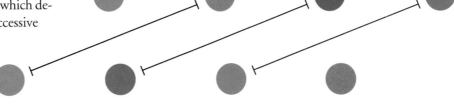

In most cases (for monitors of the same size), the smaller the dot pitch, the sharper the image. As a rule, look for a dot pitch of 0.28mm or less. If you are considering a larger monitor, such as a 17- or 21-inch monitor, a slightly larger dot pitch will produce equivalent sharpness.

UNDERSTANDING RESOLUTION

As you have learned, monitors display images by illuminating small picture elements (pixels) on your screen display. Resolution describes the number of pixels on your screen display. As a general rule, the larger a monitor's resolution, the sharper its image display. Monitor resolution is expressed in terms of *x* by *y* (horizontal by vertical) pixel counts. Common resolutions include 640×480 and 1024×768.

UNDERSTANDING INTERLACING

To display an image, the monitor constantly receives signals from the video card that tell it which colors to use for each pixel. Each time the monitor refreshes the screen (many over 70 times per second) the monitor must receive the corresponding pixel colors.

As the resolution increases, so too does the number of pixels the monitor must track. Unfortunately, some monitors simply can't keep up. In such cases, the monitors use a technique called *interlacing* when they refresh the screen. Using interlacing, the monitor refreshes every other line of pixels as it refreshes the screen.

Although interlacing lets slower monitors support higher resolutions, it can produce a wave-like screen appearance that is distracting to work at all day. If you plan to spend long hours in front of your monitor, you'll want to invest extra money and buy a non-interlaced monitor.

INTERLACED VERSUS NON-INTERLACED MONITORS

When you shop for a monitor, be aware of interlaced monitors, which display higher resolutions by refreshing every other line with each screen refresh operation. Unfortunately, by refreshing pixels in this way, interlaced monitors often produce a wave-like display. Although the lower price of the interlaced monitor may seem appealing, you won't be happy with your end result.

WHAT YOU NEED TO KNOW

As you have learned, the monitor provides only half the video picture image. The video card, which contains the electronics responsible for generating the screen image, is the other half. Lesson 20 examines video cards in detail. Before you continue with Lesson 20, however, make sure that you understand the following key concepts:

✓ Upgrading your monitor is very easy. You simply power off and unplug your system unit and your monitor. Unplug your existing monitor's power and video card cables, replacing them with your new monitor's cables.

✓ A monitor displays images on your screen by illuminating small picture elements called pixels. To illuminate the pixels, the monitor uses three electron guns.

✓ Pixels are composed of small phosphors that, when heated, illuminate in different colors. To maintain their color, phosphors must be continually refreshed (reheated). Thus, the monitor must continually move the electron guns across and down your screen. The speed at which your monitor refreshes your screen is called the monitor's refresh rate.

✓ Resolution specifies the number of pixels on your screen display. The greater the number of pixels, the sharper the images a monitor displays.

✓ Sharpness refers to the amount of space between phosphors (dot pitch). The smaller the dot pitch, the sharper the image.

✓ As a monitor's resolution increases, so too does the amount of information the monitor must handle with each screen refresh operation. Because some monitors simply can't keep up, some monitors employ a technique called interlacing. An interlaced monitor skips every other row of pixels during each screen refresh operation. Unfortunately, such interlacing can lead to a wave-like screen appearance. Be aware of interlacing when you shop for a monitor.

Lesson 20

Upgrading Your Video Card

In Lesson 19, you examined a variety of monitor characteristics and how monitors display images on your screen. If you have not yet read Lesson 19, do so now. This lesson examines video cards, which provide the first half of the video process. In short, your video card contains the electronics that tell the monitor what to display and how to display it.

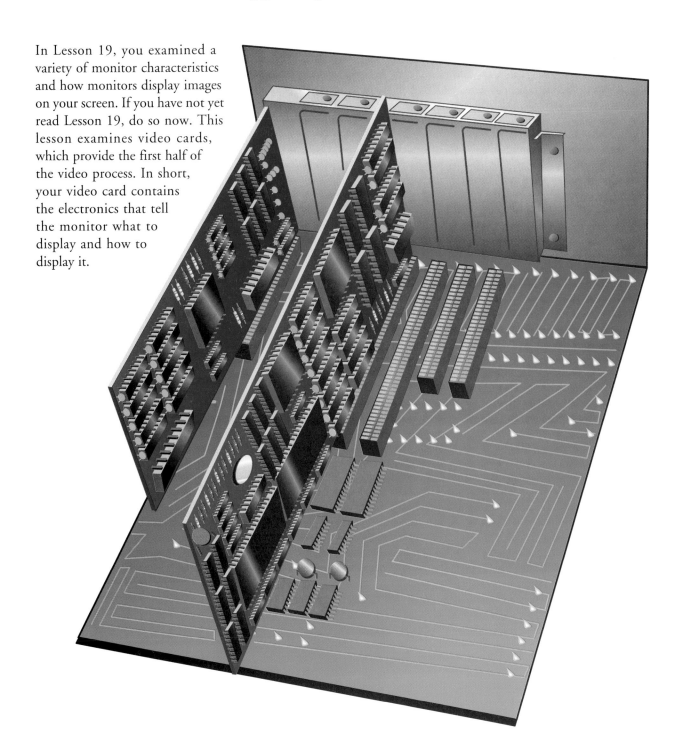

By the time you finish this lesson, you will understand the following key concepts:

- The purpose of a video accelerator

- How a video card's type controls the number of colors you can display

- The importance of video card memory

- How you might be able to get much faster performance from your existing video card or a new one at little or no extra expense

- The need for video device drivers

With the tremendous capabilities being included in multimedia programs, a fast, high-resolution, video card that supports a large number of colors is becoming a must.

WHAT YOU'LL NEED

Before you get started on this lesson, make sure that you have the following readily available:

1. A PC tool kit with a screwdriver

2. A container within which you can place the chassis screws

3. A well-lit workspace with room for you to place the chassis

4. A new video card

UNDERSTANDING THE VIDEO CARD

A video card contains the electronics that let your computer display text and graphics on your screen. In most cases, the video card resides in one of the PC's expansion slots. However, some PCs place the video card electronics directly on the motherboard. Before you can upgrade the video card for a motherboard-based video system, you will need to disable the motherboard video electronics. Normally, you will disable the motherboard video using a jumper or DIP switch, as discussed in Lesson 9.

As you know, your monitor attaches to the video card.

To display an image, the CPU sends information to the video card, which, in turn, sends the information to the monitor.

To improve your computer's video resolution or speed, normally you must replace the video card in your computer.

Before spending a lot of money on a new video card, you should make sure that your monitor can take advantage of all or most of the capabilities that the more expensive video cards offer.

UNDERSTANDING VIDEO ACCELERATORS

If you work with Windows, you are well aware that Windows succeeds by presenting commands and operations as pictures (graphics-based icons). To improve the performance of Windows, hardware developers have created enhanced video cards that accelerate common graphics-based operations. For example, a video accelerator card might have chips (processors) that Windows can take advantage of to quickly move or size a window. Likewise, the card can improve multimedia (video-based) operations by increasing the rate at which the screen can be updated. If you are shopping for a "fast" PC, make sure that you purchase a video accelerator.

HOW VIDEO CARDS DIFFER

As you shop for video cards, you will find that cards differ greatly in price. In addition, video cards can differ in three other ways:

- The card's speed (accelerated or not)
- The number of colors the card can display
- The card's resolution

If you make extensive use of Windows or other graphics-based programs, you will find that a video accelerator card significantly improves your system performance. In the near future, as more multimedia applications include video, an accelerator card will be a must.

As you learned in Lesson 19, monitors display images by illuminating small phosphor dots called pixels. Resolution specifies the number of pixels that appear on the screen display. The higher a card's resolution, the greater the number of pixels and the sharper the screen image.

A video card also defines the number of colors your monitor can use to display an image. Video cards are often classified as 8-bit, 16-bit, or 24-bit cards, based on the number of bits the card uses to represent each pixel's color. Table 20.1 lists the number of colors these video card types can display.

Video Card	Number of Colors
8-bit	256
16-bit	65,536
24-bit	16,777,216

Table 20.1 The number of colors different video cards can display.

When you shop for video cards, you need to be careful. The ideal video card has a high resolution and can display a large number of colors at that resolution. Be aware of advertisements that state a card can display over 16 million colors. Instead, look for cards that can display over 16 million colors with a high resolution, such as 800 × 600 or even 1280 × 1024. The key factor in determining how many colors a video card can display at different resolutions is the card's onboard memory.

As you shop, you will encounter video cards that have varying amounts of onboard memory (normally 1Mb or 2Mb). Within its onboard memory, the video card holds a color value for each pixel. If your monitor is running with 1280 x 1024 resolution, the card must hold values for 1,310,720 pixels. If the card can display 256 colors, each pixel color requires eight bits or one byte. If the card can display 65,536 colors, each pixel color requires 16 bits or two bytes. In this case, the card's video memory must hold 2,621,440 bytes. Finally, to display over 16 million colors, each pixel color requires 24 bits (or three bytes) and the card's memory would have to hold 3,932,160 bytes! As you can see, the amount of onboard memory a video card contains, defines the number of colors the card can display at different resolutions.

FASTER VIDEO PERFORMANCE INEXPENSIVELY

As you have read, video cards come with onboard memory, sometimes as much as 4Mb. They also have their own BIOS (Basic Input/Output System), which resides in onboard ROM. Unfortunately, the video BIOS ROM is quite slow, compared to your computer's fast RAM (Random Access Memory). As a result, many video cards have, on the software disk that accompanies the card, a utility program (perhaps named something like RAMBIOS.EXE), that copies the card's video BIOS to the faster RAM of your computer.

When you run such a program, every activity involving video output will be faster. Many computer users already have such a program and are unaware of it. Read the user's manual for your video card to see if you can benefit from this "free ride."

INSTALLING A VIDEO CARD

To replace your existing video card, power off and unplug your PC system unit. Unplug your monitor from the video card. Remove your system unit cover, as discussed in Lesson 2, and discharge any static electricity from your body. Locate and remove your existing video card—it's the card into which your monitor was plugged. If your video electronics reside on the motherboard, you will need to disable the electronics, as you read earlier. To determine the actual steps you must perform to disable motherboard electronics, refer to the documentation that accompanied your PC.

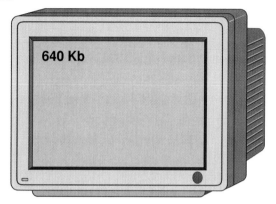

Next, gently slide and secure the new video card into an expansion slot. Replace your system unit cover. Attach your monitor to the new video card. Plug in and power on your PC. As your system starts, you should see a count of your system's memory on the screen display.

If the memory count appears, your video card installation was successful. If the memory count does not appear, first ensure that you have correctly cabled the card to your monitor and that your monitor is plugged in. Second, double-check that you have securely inserted the video card within the expansion slot. Next, your video card might conflict with another card. You might need to remove one or more cards until you identify the source of the conflict. If the error persists, you should contact your retailer or the card's technical support staff.

INSTALLING A VIDEO CARD

To install a video card, perform the following steps:

1. Power off and unplug your PC system unit.

2. Unplug your monitor from the current video card.

3. Remove your system unit cover and discharge any static from your body.

4. Remove your existing video card.

5. Insert and secure the new video card into an expansion slot.

6. Replace the system unit cover.

7. Plug in and power on your PC.

UNDERSTANDING VIDEO CARD TYPES

When you shop for a video card, you need to purchase a card that is compatible with your PC's expansion slots. Many video cards, for example, use a local bus to improve their performance. Unfortunately, if your PC does not have a local bus, you can't take advantage of such boards. Lesson 4 examines PC expansion slots in detail. Before you shop for a video card, read through Lesson 4.

UNDERSTANDING VIDEO CARD DEVICE DRIVERS

In Lesson 28, you will examine device drivers, which are special software programs that let Windows or DOS use a hardware device. By default, DOS and your PC BIOS provide support for basic devices such as the keyboard, screen, and printer. As you add devices (perhaps a mouse, scanner, or CD-ROM), you will need to install device driver software. If you purchase a video accelerator card, you might need to install a device driver for DOS, as well as Windows. If you don't install the device driver, your system might still be able to use the card. However, your system will probably use the card in its most basic ways, failing to take advantage of an accelerator or increased resolution.

When you purchase a video card, you will normally receive a floppy disk that contains DOS and Windows device drivers for the card. The documentation that accompanies your video card will specify the steps you must perform to install the device driver. For more information on how to tell Windows about a new device, turn to Lesson 29.

WHAT YOU NEED TO KNOW

With rapid increase of public interest in graphics, multimedia presentation, and animation, video card upgrades are becoming a must-have option to take full advantage of these fields and modern monitors. In this chapter you have learned how to upgrade your video card.

Over the next year more than five million users will install CD-ROM drives in their systems. In Lesson 18, you will learn how to install a CD-ROM drive. Before you continue with Lesson 18, however, make sure that you have learned the following key concepts:

✓ A video accelerator is an expansion slot card that contains special processing chips that can speed up different video operations. As the number of Windows-based multimedia programs increases, video accelerators will become standard equipment.

✓ Different video card types support different capabilities (resolutions and colors). If you are concerned about system performance, you should begin your search with only those video cards that include an accelerator. However, such video cards are significantly more expensive than their slower counterparts.

✓ Video cards contain their own memory, which actually stores the image that is displayed on the screen. The more memory a video card contains, the more colors the card can display at one time.

✓ If the software disk that came with your video card includes a program (perhaps named something like RAMBIOS.EXE), that copies the video BIOS from the card's relatively slow onboard ROM to the computer's fast RAM, you get faster performance from every operation that involves video output by running that program. Check your card's user manual.

✓ Depending on your video card type, you might have to install special device driver software before Windows can take advantage of the card's capabilities.

Lesson 21

Installing a CD-ROM Drive

With the explosive growth of multimedia-based software, it is estimated that over five million users will install a CD-ROM drive this year alone! This lesson examines the different CD-ROM drive types and the steps you must perform to install each. By the time you finish this lesson, you will understand the following key concepts:

- CD-ROM drives can connect to a sound card or SCSI adapter
- CD-ROM drives can be internal or external
- CD-ROM drives come in different speeds
- Before you can use a CD-ROM drive, you must install device driver software

WHAT YOU'LL NEED

Before you get started on this lesson, make sure that you have the following readily available:

1. A PC tool kit with a screwdriver
2. A container within which you can place the chassis screws and a container for drive slot screws
3. A well-lit workspace with room for you to place the chassis and drive
4. A new CD-ROM drive and cables

SHOPPING FOR A CD-ROM DRIVE

If you have not yet purchased a CD-ROM, consider the following factors as your shopping guide:

Cost   As you shop, you will find that the cost of CD-ROM drives can differ considerably. Normally, the major factor affecting CD-ROM drive cost is drive speed. A triple-speed drive will cost considerably more than a double-speed drive. Unfortunately, if you wait for the cost of triple-speed drives to come down, you'll then have the same dilemma with quadruple-speed drives. The second factor affecting drive cost is whether the drive is an internal or external drive. You will normally pay more for an external drive because of the cost of the case and wiring and because you can quickly move the drive from one system to another.

Speed   CD-ROM drives differ in speed. The original drives transferred data at a rate of 150Kbs (approximately 150,000 bytes per second). Today, double-speed drives transfer data at 300Kbs and triple-speed drives at 450Kbs. If you are using multimedia programs that display video, the faster your drive, the better your video quality. As a rule, do not buy a drive slower than 300Kbs. If you plan to hold on to your drive for some time, spend extra money now and buy a faster drive.

Internal versus External   You can install a CD-ROM drive within one of your system unit drive bay slots or you can use an external drive. The advantage of an external drive is that you can easily move the drive from one computer to another. In fact, you can now connect CD-ROM drives to many notebook computers using a PCMCIA card. If you have multiple computers, you might want to consider an external CD-ROM drive.

SCSI versus non-SCSI   A CD-ROM drive can connect to either a SCSI adapter or to a sound card. The advantage of a SCSI-based CD-ROM drive is that the drive is not tied to your sound card. Should you decide to replace a sound card that provides the drive interface, you might be forced to replace the drive itself (a costly proposition). In addition, a SCSI drive is easier to move from one system to another.

Multimedia Upgrade Kit   Most CD-ROM drives sold today are packaged in a multimedia upgrade kit that also provides a sound card, speakers, and several sample CDs. Many stores offer aggressive pricing on multimedia upgrade kits. However, before you purchase an upgrade kit, make sure that the CD-ROM drive and sound card provided meet your needs. Otherwise, purchase both separately. If you want a SCSI-based CD-ROM drive, make sure the kit provides one.

BE AWARE OF CD-ROM DRIVES THAT CONNECT TO SOUND CARDS

If your CD-ROM drive connects to a sound card, you might only be able to use the drive with a specific type of sound card. If you should some day change your sound card, you might not be able to use your drive! The problem is that many sound cards use proprietary electronics to connect the drive. Thus, you might not be able to plug your drive into a different sound card or into a SCSI adapter.

If you have not yet purchased a CD-ROM drive, you should strongly consider a SCSI-based drive. In this way, should you ever change sound cards, you can continue to use your existing drive.

CONNECTING A CD-ROM DRIVE

Depending on your CD-ROM drive type, you connect the drive to either a sound card or SCSI adapter. If you have purchased a multimedia upgrade kit, your drive will very likely connect to the sound card in the kit.

As you can see, CD-ROM drives can be internal (residing within a drive bay in the system unit) or external. The steps you must perform to install an internal or external drive will differ, as discussed next.

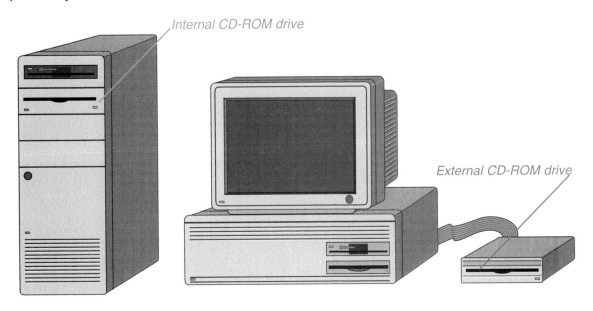

Internal CD-ROM drive

External CD-ROM drive

Note: The next two sections tell you how to install an internal or an external CD-ROM. If you don't already have a SCSI adapter card or the proper sound board installed, you will need to install one. Lesson 5 describes installation of hardware cards in general, Lesson 15 describes installation of a SCSI adapter, and Lesson 18 describes installation of a multimedia sound card.

INSTALLING AN INTERNAL CD-ROM DRIVE

To install an internal CD-ROM drive, power off and unplug your PC's system unit. Next, remove the system unit cover, as discussed in Lesson 2, and discharge any static from your body. Locate the drive bay into which you will insert the drive. Remove the drive bay screws so you can later use the screws to secure the drive in place. If you are replacing an existing drive with the CD-ROM, first remove the ribbon cable that connects the drive to the controller. Next, remove the power cable that connects the drive to the power supply.

Note: If your PC's drive bay does not contain rails into which you will slide the drive, you can buy the rails at your computer retailer. If your PC needs drive rails, you might find it easier to let your computer retailer complete the installation for you.

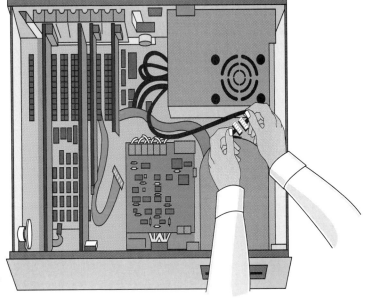

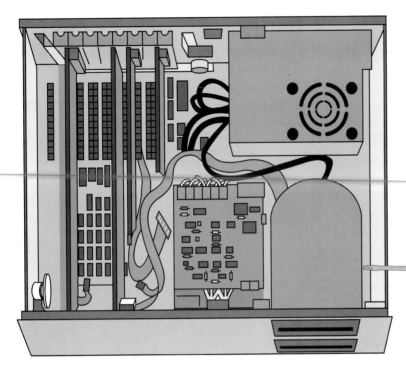

After you slide the CD-ROM drive into place, secure the drive to the drive bay using the screws you previously removed.

Next, use the ribbon cable that accompanied your drive to connect to either the sound card or the SCSI adapter.

Connect the power supply cable to the drive.

Replace the system unit cover and plug in and power on your PC.

Note: If you are connecting the drive to a SCSI adapter, you might need to set the drive's SCSI address, as discussed in Lesson 15. Also, depending on the drive's location in the SCSI daisy chain, you might need to terminate the CD-ROM drive.

INSTALLING AN EXTERNAL CD-ROM DRIVE

Installing an external CD-ROM drive is actually quite simple. To begin, power off and unplug your PC system unit. Next, using the ribbon cable that accompanied the drive, connect the drive to the corresponding adapter. Next, you must plug in the drive to a power outlet.

Note: If you are connecting the drive to a SCSI adapter, you may need to set the SCSI address of the drive as discussed in Lesson 15. Also, depending on the drive's location in the SCSI daisy chain, you may need to terminate the CD-ROM drive.

INSTALLING THE DRIVE'S DEVICE DRIVER SOFTWARE

Before DOS or Windows can access the CD-ROM drive, you must first install special device driver software. The documentation that accompanied your drive will specify the steps you must perform to install the device driver software. Likewise, a floppy disk that contains the device driver should have accompanied your drive.

Normally, you will run an installation program that automatically updates your AUTOEXEC.BAT or CONFIG.SYS files, inserting the necessary commands or statements required to load the device driver each time your computer starts. After the installation program ends, you might need to restart your system. In addition to providing an installation program, the floppy disk might include one or more test programs you can run to ensure that you have correctly installed the CD-ROM drive.

Note: If your CD-ROM drive connects to a sound card, first ensure that your sound card is properly working before you start troubleshooting the CD-ROM drive itself.

CD-ROM DRIVES COME IN DIFFERENT SPEEDS

When CD-ROM drives were first released, the drives could transmit up to 150,000 bytes (150Kb) of information per second. Today, most drives can transmit up to 300,000 bytes per second. These are referred to as *double-speed drives*. As more multimedia programs begin to use video, the speed of your CD-ROM drive becomes very important. The faster the drive, the more information the drive can provide to the computer in a short period of time. The larger the amounts of transmitted video data, for example, the more realistic the video's appearance. Recently, the price of triple-speed drives (450Kb/second) has begun to drop. When you shop for a CD-ROM drive, you need to consider the drive's speed.

WHAT YOU NEED TO KNOW

The vast amount of information that can fit on one CD-ROM makes it an excellent candidate for applications that require a lot of storage space, such as animation, detailed graphics, and sound. In this lesson, you have learned how to install a CD-ROM drive.

When you plug in your PC system unit, you actually plug in the PC's power supply, which, in turn, disseminates power to the electronic components within your PC. Occasionally, a power supply will fail and you must replace it. In Lesson 22, you will examine the steps you must perform to replace a power supply. Before you continue with Lesson 22, however, make sure that you have learned the following key concepts:

- ✓ CD-ROM drives can be internal or external.

- ✓ You can connect a CD-ROM drive to a sound card or SCSI adapter, depending on the type of drive.

- ✓ Be aware of CD-ROM drives that connect to a sound card. If you ever change sound cards, you might not be able to use your CD-ROM drive.

- ✓ CD-ROM drives come in different speeds. The faster the CD-ROM drive, the more information the drive can provide the computer in a short period of time. If you are shopping for a CD-ROM drive, you should consider a triple-speed drive or faster.

Lesson 22

Replacing the PC's Power Supply

Every operation the PC performs is based on the presence or absence of electronic signals. When you plug your PC's power into your 120-volt AC (alternating current) wall socket, you actually plug in the PC's power supply. The power supply transforms the voltage into the 5-volt DC (direct current) that the computer can use. Within your PC's system unit, in turn, other devices such as the motherboard and disk drives plug into the power supply. Occasionally, a power supply will fail, and you will need to replace it. This lesson covers the steps you must perform to replace a power supply. By the time you finish this lesson, you will understand the following key concepts:

- How to recognize a failed power supply
- How to replace your power supply
- How and when you need to plug devices into your power supply
- How to determine your PC's power requirements

When the original IBM PC was released in 1981, the PC shipped with a small 63-watt power supply. Since many internal hardware devices require power, many users replaced their power supplies to put in a larger power supply. Today, most PCs ship with large power supplies (200 watts or more) which should more than meet your PC's needs.

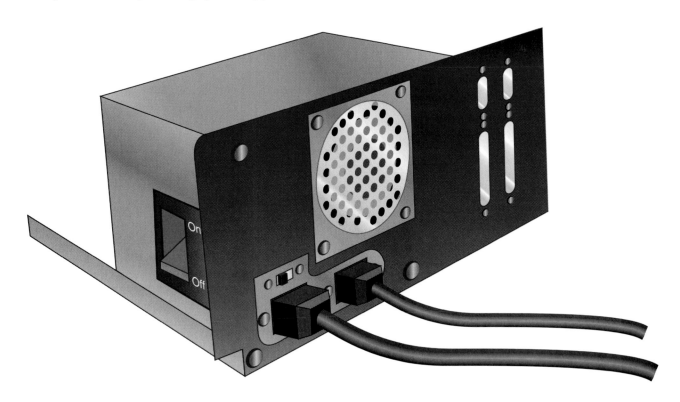

RECOGNIZING A FAILED POWER SUPPLY

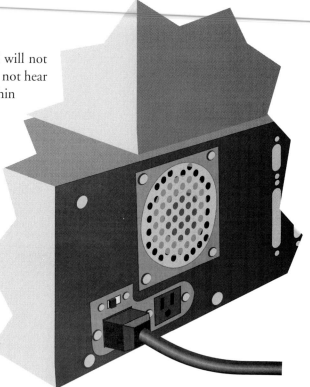

When your PC's power supply does not work, the PC will not start. In addition, when the power supply fails, you will not hear the PC's fan whir. As you can see, the fan is contained within the power supply.

Don't jump to the assumption that your power supply is bad just because your system does not start and you cannot hear the fan whir. Instead, first double-check the PC's power plugs to ensure that they are plugged in correctly. Next, verify that the wall outlet into which the PC is plugged is working.

If you are using a surge suppresser, as discussed in Lesson 1, remove the suppresser and plug your PC directly into a working wall outlet. When a surge suppresser captures an electrical spike, it will normally trip an internal breaker. Most surge suppressers have a reset button you can press to restore the suppressor's normal operation.

REPLACING YOUR POWER SUPPLY

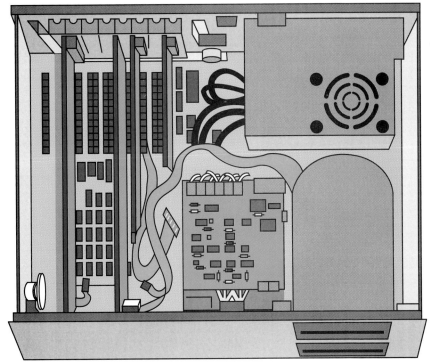

To replace your PC's power supply, first power off and unplug the PC system unit.

Next, remove the system unit cover, as discussed in Lesson 2.

Place the screws you remove in a safe location.

As discussed, the PC motherboard and disk drives plug into the power supply.

Locate the small power supply cables and their plugs.

To remove the plugs, you might need to rock the plugs gently from right to left.

Be careful to grasp the plugs and not the wires attached to the plugs or you might damage the power supply cables.

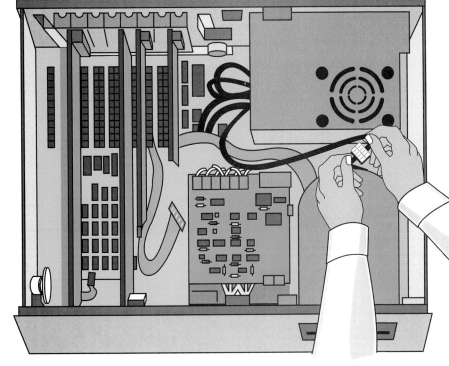

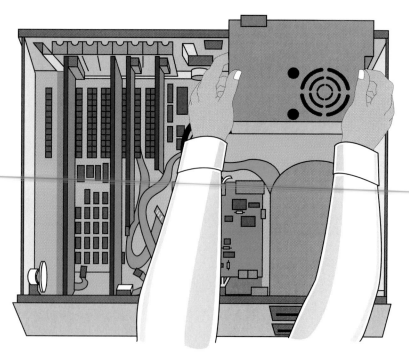

There are normally several screws that hold the power supply to the back of the system unit. Remove these screws and place them in a safe location.

The power supply should now lift out from your system unit easily. Be careful as you lift the power supply from the system unit.

The power supply can be deceptively heavily. Make sure you do not set the power supply (or let it fall, in the case of a tower configuration) on top of any fragile components.

Place your new power supply into the system unit and replace the screws that attach the power supply to the system unit.

Next, plug in your motherboard, disk drives, and other devices you may have unplugged from the power supply.

Note that the power supply plugs are shaped such that they can only be plugged in one way.

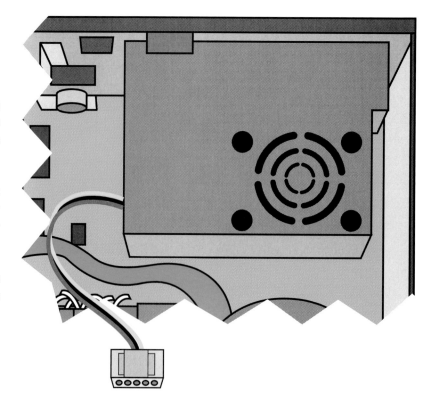

REPLACING A POWER SUPPLY

To replace a power supply, perform these steps:

1. Power off and unplug the system unit.
2. Remove the system unit cover, as discussed in Lesson 2.
3. Unplug devices attached to power supply cables, such as your motherboard and disk drives.
4. Remove the screws that attach the power supply to the system unit. Place the screws in a safe location.
5. Lift your old power supply from the system unit, replacing it with the new power supply.
6. Secure the power supply within your system unit by replacing the screws you previously removed.
7. Plug in the devices you previously unplugged from the power supply.
8. Replace and secure your system unit cover.
9. Plug in and power on your PC.

WHICH DEVICES PLUG INTO THE POWER SUPPLY

As you have learned, your PC's motherboard and your disk drives plug into the power supply. As you read through the lessons in this book, you might install other devices such as a CD-ROM or tape drive that you must also plug into the power supply. As a rule, you will normally need to plug in larger mechanical devices. Cards such as a sound board or modem, on the other hand, do not need to be plugged in. Instead, these devices get their power directly from the expansion slot.

SPLITTING A POWER SUPPLY CABLE

Depending on the devices you install within your system unit, there may be times when you run out of power supply cables before the power supply runs out of available power.

In such cases, you can use a power cable splitter, which breaks one power cable into two.

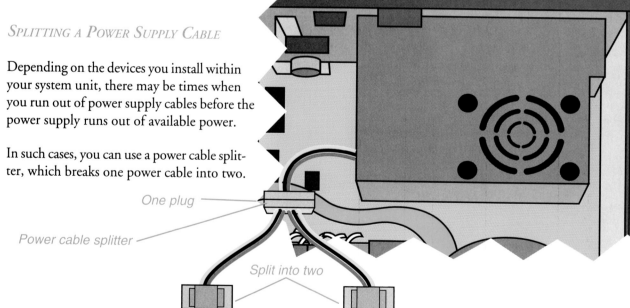

One plug

Power cable splitter

Split into two

HOW TO DETERMINE YOUR POWER REQUIREMENTS

As you have learned, most power supplies sold today provide 200 watts. To determine your PC's power requirements, use the device power needs listed in Table 22.1.

Device	Power Requirement
CD-ROM drive	20 to 25 watts
Expansion board (small card)	5 watts
Expansion slots (large card)	10 to 15 watts
Floppy drive (3 1/2-inch)	5 watts
Floppy drive (5 1/4-inch)	5 to 15 watts
Hard drive (3 1/2-inch)	5 to 15 watts
Hard drive (5 1/4-inch)	10 to 30 watts
Memory (per Mb)	5 watts
Motherboard	20 to 35 watts

Table 22.1 Power requirements for common PC devices.

WHAT YOU NEED TO KNOW

As the number of hardware devices in your computer increases, so too does the amount of power required of your power supply. In this lesson, you have learned how much power various devices use and how to replace your power supply.

With the tremendous success and popularity of Microsoft Windows, a mouse is becoming almost as prevalent as a keyboard. Lesson 23 examines the different PC mouse types and the steps you must perform to upgrade your mouse. Before you continue with Lesson 23, however, make sure that you understand the following key concepts:

✓ When you plug in your PC, you actually plug in the PC's power supply. The power supply, in turn, disperses power throughout your PC's internal components.

✓ When your power supply fails, not only will your PC not start, you will not hear the power supply's built-in fan.

✓ Before you blame your PC's power supply, make sure you first double-check your power cables and surge suppressor and ensure that the wall outlet is working.

✓ Power requirements are expressed in terms of watts. Today, most power supplies sold provide 200 watts of power.

Lesson 23

Upgrading Your Mouse

With the tremendous success and acceptance of Microsoft Windows, virtually every PC sold today ships with a mouse. Because a mouse is a mechanical device, it can eventually wear out. This lesson examines the steps you must perform to replace a mouse. In addition, this lesson presents several concepts you might want to consider when shopping for a mouse. By the time you finish this lesson, you will understand the following key concepts:

- There are three primary mouse types: a serial, bus, and proprietary mouse

- Mice differ by the number of buttons they support and their resolution

- A wireless mouse eliminates the mouse cable—an optical mouse eliminates the ball

- A trackball is like a stationary, upside-down mouse with a large ball—very handy if desk space is limited

- The mouse's use and the functions it is capable of performing are defined by the mouse driver

- When you upgrade your mouse, you need to inform your software

WHAT YOU'LL NEED

Depending on your mouse type, you might have to open your system unit. If you are installing a bus mouse and bus mouse card, make sure you have the following readily available before you get started on this lesson.

1. A PC tool kit with a screwdriver
2. A container within which you can place the chassis screws
3. A well lit workspace with room for you to place the chassis

UNDERSTANDING HOW YOUR MOUSE WORKS

As you know, when you move a mouse across your desk, a mouse cursor moves in the same way across your screen.

If you turn the mouse over, you will find the mouse ball. As you move the mouse, this ball's movement causes the mouse to produce signals which, in turn, move the cursor.

For the computer to respond to mouse movements, the mouse must be connected to the computer. There are three ways to connect a mouse to your computer. These connection techniques correspond to the three mouse types: serial, bus, and proprietary mice.

USING A SERIAL MOUSE

A *serial mouse* is a mouse that connects to one of your computer's serial ports, such as COM1 or COM2. The serial mouse is the most commonly used mouse. To replace a serial mouse, simply unplug your current mouse and plug in the new mouse.

The advantage of a serial mouse is its simplicity. Windows and other software programs readily support most serial mice. In fact, most serial mice conform to the Microsoft mouse standard. Thus, when you tell your software that you are using a serial mouse, you might be able to use the Microsoft mouse type if your mouse is not listed in the supported mice.

The disadvantage of a serial mouse is that the mouse consumes a serial port that you might need to use for a modem, printer, or other device.

Slide the tape drive into the drive bay. Secure the tape unit in place with the screws you previously removed from the system unit rails. Next, attach a power cable from the PC's power supply to the tape unit.

Internal tape drives connect to the PC in one of three ways. First, the tape unit might use its own controller card. If this is the case, use the MSD command to determine a proper IRQ setting for the card. Change the board settings if necessary. Insert the card into an expansion slot and use the tape drive's ribbon cable to connect the controller and tape unit.

Second, the tape unit might connect to a SCSI adapter. In this case, connect the tape drive ribbon cable to a SCSI adapter or to a device in the SCSI device chain (see Lesson 9). Finally, some tape drives connect to the floppy disk controller with a special ribbon cable. The documentation that accompanied your tape unit will tell you the steps you must perform.

After the tape unit is connected to a controller, replace the system unit cover and plug in and power on your PC.

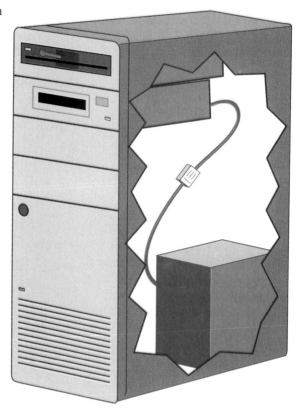

Installing an External Tape Drive

External tape units connect to the PC in one of three ways. First, the drive might connect to its own controller card. If you must install a controller card, power off and unplug your PC. Follow the steps discussed in Lesson 3 to install the card. After the card is properly installed and the system unit cover is in place, connect the tape drive to the card and plug in the tape drive. Next, plug in and power on your PC system unit.

Second, the external tape drive might connect to a SCSI adapter. If you must install the SCSI adapter card, follow the steps presented in Lesson 9. If the SCSI card is already in place, power off your PC and SCSI peripherals. Connect the tape unit to the adapter or the SCSI daisy chain. Plug in your tape drive unit, the system unit, and your SCSI peripherals.

Finally, some tape drives connect to a PC parallel port such as LPT1. To connect a tape drive to a parallel port, power off your PC. If necessary, remove the cable for a device currently connected to the parallel port. Next, connect the tape unit to the parallel port. Plug in the tape unit and power on the PC.

Using Tape Drive Software

Tape drives normally come with software that lets you test the tape drive and perform backup operations. The documentation that accompanied your tape drive should discuss the software in detail. In addition, there are several third-party tape drive backup programs available on the market that you might find easier to use.

Spend More and Purchase Formatted Tapes

When you purchase tapes for your tape drive, you can purchase unformatted or formatted tapes. The formatted tapes will be a little more expensive. However, formatting tapes is a time-consuming task. The money you save by purchasing an unformatted tape is probably not worth the time you will spend formatting tapes.

What You Need to Know

The dramatic increase in hard disk sizes has made floppy disk-based backup unfeasibly slow. Fortunately, the advances in hard disk technology have been paralleled by advances in backup technology. In this lesson, you have learned how to install a tape drive into your system.

Most users make extensive use of their printers. However, most never think about upgrading their printers. As you will learn in Lesson 25, you can improve your system performance by upgrading your printer. Before you continue with Lesson 25, however, make sure you understand the following key concepts:

✓ Tape drives make it very easy to perform disk backups. In addition, you can normally perform an unattended tape backup in much less time than a floppy disk-based backup.

✓ Tape drives can be internal or external devices.

✓ Internal tape drives can be connected to a SCSI adapter, a proprietary card, or a floppy disk controller card.

✓ External tape drives connect to a SCSI adapter, a proprietary card, or a parallel port.

✓ Most tape drives come with software that you can use to test your tape drive installation and to back up the files on your disk.

Lesson 25

Upgrading Your Printer

Because of the large number of printer types, it is difficult, at best, to list the exact steps you must perform to upgrade different parts of your printer. Instead, this lesson examines several common printer upgrades and the benefits each offers. By the time you finish this lesson, you will understand the following key concepts:

- If you can connect a given printer to a parallel or serial port, using a parallel port significantly improves your system performance

- Adding memory to your printer improves your system performance

- Printers use hard and soft fonts

- PostScript is a programming language for printers

- Using Windows, you can choose system performance over printer performance or vice versa

CHOOSING A SERIAL OR PARALLEL PORT

Most printers provide serial and parallel ports. Serial ports are normally used for slower devices that don't transmit very large amounts of data in short periods of time, such as a mouse. Serial ports transmit data one *bit* (*b*inary dig*it*) at a time on a single wire. Parallel ports, on the other hand, transmit data over eight wires at the same time. As a result, parallel ports are much faster.

If you examine your printer closely, you should find a serial port and a parallel port. If you are using the serial port, you will improve your system performance by upgrading to a parallel port connection.

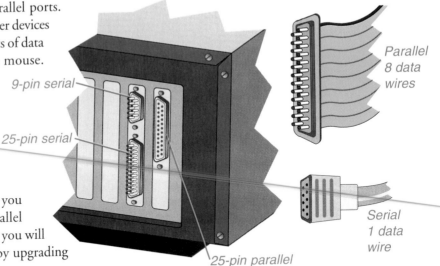

9-pin serial

25-pin serial

25-pin parallel

Parallel 8 data wires

Serial 1 data wire

*Note: If you change your printer connection from a serial port to a parallel port, you will need to tell Windows and possibly other programs that you are now using a parallel port. For information on changing the Windows printer used, turn to the book **Rescued by Windows**, Jamsa Press, 1993. Also, depending on your printer type, you might need to change your printer setup to use the parallel port.*

WHY PARALLEL PORTS IMPROVE YOUR SYSTEM PERFORMANCE

When your program writes data to the printer, your program must wait until the printer has received all the data into its memory. Even if you are using a print spooler, like the Windows Print Manager, to transfer the data in the background, your program will run slower until all of the data is transferred because the spooler and your program must share the CPU.

If you are using a serial port, your computer transmits the data one bit a time, a slow process. Parallel ports, on the other hand, transmit data eight bits at a time, a much faster process. By reducing the amount of time it takes for your programs to send information to the printer, your programs become more responsive. As a result, your system performance is improved.

ADDING PRINTER MEMORY

When you print a document, your application program sends the document to the printer, which, in turn, places the document into its own memory. The printer then prints the information its memory contains. If your document is small, the entire document will fit into your printer's memory. In this way, the application does not have to wait for the entire document to print before it can continue. Once the printer's memory contains the document, the application considers the printing complete and can continue other operations.

If the document you are printing is larger than the printer's memory, the application must wait for the printer to print part of the document so it can send more data to the printer. This waiting and sending process continues until the last of the document is in the printer's memory.

By adding memory to your printer, you increase the likelihood that your documents can fit into the printer's memory. In this way, you reduce the amount of time your applications spend waiting on the printer. Depending on your printer type, the steps you must perform to install memory will differ. If you are using an older printer, the printer memory very likely resides on a hardware card. Newer printers, on the other hand, use SIMM chips similar to those discussed in Lesson 13.

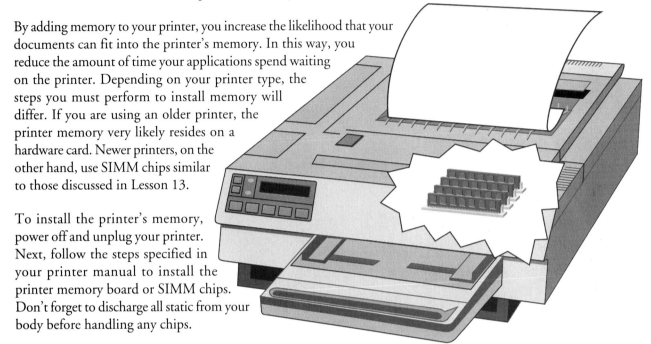

To install the printer's memory, power off and unplug your printer. Next, follow the steps specified in your printer manual to install the printer memory board or SIMM chips. Don't forget to discharge all static from your body before handling any chips.

Note: Most printers provide a menu option or button combination that lets you print a printer status report page specifying the amount of memory the printer contains, a list of built-in fonts, and even the number of pages the printer has printed to date. For specifics on printing your printer's status page, refer to the documentation that accompanied your printer.

ADDING PRINTER MEMORY

By adding memory to your printer, you increase the likelihood that your printer can hold the documents you print. In this way, you decrease the amount of time your programs spend waiting on the printer. To install memory within your printer, perform these steps:

1. Power off and unplug your printer.

2. Follow the steps specified in the manual that accompanied your printer to install the memory board or SIMM chips.

3. Plug in and power on your printer.

ADDING PRINTER FONTS

Most printers come with a collection of built-in fonts. Using an option on a printer menu or by pressing a button combination on your printer, you should be able to display the printer's current fonts. For specifics on printing a font sample, refer to the documentation that accompanied your printer.

Printer fonts are classified as hard or soft. *Hard fonts* are built into the printer or reside in an add-on font cartridge. *Soft fonts*, on the other hand, are provided on disk, much like software. When you use a soft font, your program loads the font into the printer's memory (another good reason to install more memory into your printer—to make room for documents with many soft fonts). Today, most users make extensive use of soft fonts, such as the TrueType fonts provided with Windows. For more information on using soft fonts with Windows, turn to *Rescued by Windows*, Jamsa Press, 1993.

The most common way to increase the number of hard fonts in your printer is to install a font cartridge. A font cartridge is just that—a small memory-board cartridge that you insert into a socket in your printer. Each cartridge contains one or more font families. In most cases, you cannot use the font cartridge for one type of printer in a second printer type.

UNDERSTANDING POSTSCRIPT

As you have learned, a computer program is simply a list of instructions the computer executes. Computer programs are written in a programming language such as C++, BASIC, Pascal, and so on. In a similar way, PostScript is a programming language for printers. Using PostScript, you can create powerful effects such as those shown here:

... a computer user's best friend

In this case, we created these designs by writing our own PostScript programs. Within the PostScript programs, we specified the instructions the printer should perform to create the designs. If you have a PostScript printer, many applications will take advantage of PostScript's programming capabilities behind the scenes. If you perform considerable desktop publishing or if you create computer-based illustrations, you will probably work with PostScript files on a regular basis, and you will want a PostScript printer. If you only use your printer to print word processing or spreadsheet documents, you probably don't need PostScript capabilities.

In the past, PostScript printers were very expensive. Thus, some users would add special hardware to their printers that added PostScript capabilities. With PostScript printers becoming more affordable, you should buy a new printer if you need PostScript support. In most cases, a newer printer will provide faster output (print more pages per minute) and give you higher resolution (sharper images).

Printer Performance and Windows

When you use Windows, you can choose between printer and system performance. Normally, when you print a document within Windows, a special program called the Print Manager runs and oversees the document's printing. Because the Print Manager oversees the document's printing in the background, your program is free to continue. As you resume your work with the program or other programs, the Print Manager will continue its work in the background, printing your document.

The Print Manager's goal is to print your documents in a timely manner without slowing down your system as you work. As a rule, the Print Manager does this pretty well. Some users, however, have specific desires—they either want their documents to print very quickly or they want maximum system performance, letting their documents print as time permits. To satisfy different users, the Print Manager lets you prioritize printing versus system performance. Windows also lets you turn the Print Manager off (this is sometimes necessary when you print extremely large files, such as large scanned images at high resolutions). When the Print Manager is off, your applications cannot continue their work until the entire document they are printing resides completely in the printer's memory. For specifics on how you can control the Print Manager, turn to *Rescued by Windows*, Jamsa Press, 1993.

What You Need to Know

Printing is a process that almost every computer user does. As a result, almost every user can benefit by a printer upgrade of some kind. In this lesson, you have learned several ways to improve your printer performance.

To many users, the keyboard has become an extension of their fingertips. However, few users think about upgrading their keyboards. In Lesson 26, you will examine different keyboard upgrades. Before you continue with Lesson 26, however, make sure that you understand the following key concepts:

✓ You can connect many printers to either a serial or parallel port. If you connect such a printer to a parallel port, you will have much better performance.

✓ Just as you can improve your PC performance by adding memory to your PC, you can also improve your system performance by adding memory to your printer.

✓ Depending on your printer type, its memory can come on a hardware card or on SIMM chips. Refer to the documentation that accompanied your printer to determine the steps you must perform to install additional memory.

✓ Printers can use hard or soft fonts. Hard fonts are built into your printer or a font cartridge. Soft fonts, on the other hand, come on disk. When a program uses soft fonts, the program downloads the font into the printer's memory.

✓ PostScript is a printer programming language. If you perform considerable desktop publishing or create computer-based illustrations, you will probably work with PostScript files on a regular basis and will want a PostScript printer—otherwise, you probably won't need PostScript capabilities.

✓ When you print documents within Windows, a special program called the Print Manager oversees the document printing. Using the Print Manager, you can prioritize your printer and system performance.

Lesson 26

Upgrading Your Keyboard

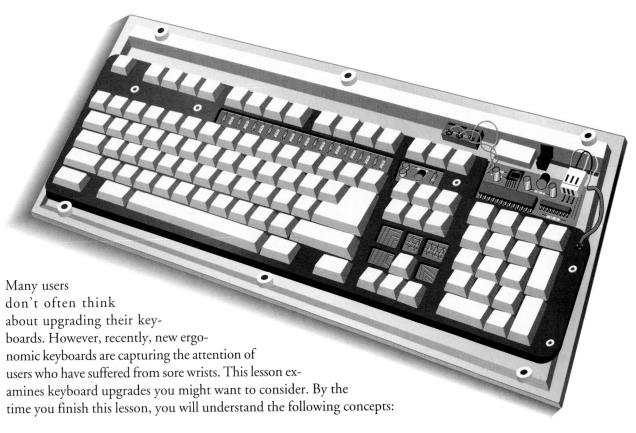

Many users
don't often think
about upgrading their keyboards. However, recently, new ergonomic keyboards are capturing the attention of
users who have suffered from sore wrists. This lesson examines keyboard upgrades you might want to consider. By the
time you finish this lesson, you will understand the following concepts:

- The purpose of the keyboard controller

- How the keyboard controller simplifies a keyboard
  upgrade

- The advantage of ergonomic keyboards

- How keyboard pads can reduce wrist strain

UNDERSTANDING THE KEYBOARD CONTROLLER

A keyboard controller is the electronic chip that converts the
keystrokes you type into the electronic signals the PC understands.
The keyboard controller resides within the keyboard itself.

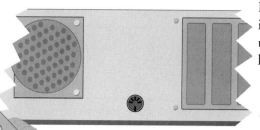

Because keyboards essentially "bring their own electronics," it is very easy for you to upgrade your keyboard. In short, to upgrade your keyboard, you simply unplug your existing keyboard and plug in your new keyboard.

UNDERSTANDING KEYBOARD ERGONOMICS

For many users, the keyboard has become an extension of their fingers. Unfortunately, for many users, existing keyboard designs have led to sore wrists, tendonitis, and even carpal-tunnel syndrome. As a result, newer keyboard designs have emerged that reduce the stress on your wrists and hands.

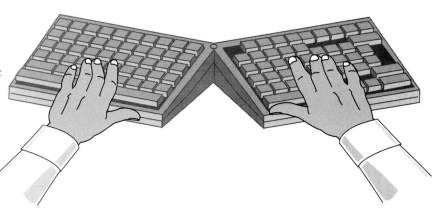

As the price of these ergonomic keyboards continues to drop, more users will make the switch.

To take advantage of these keyboards, you simply power off your PC, unplug your existing keyboard, and replace it with the new keyboard.

PUTTING A WRIST PAD TO WORK

If you are not quite ready to spring for an ergonomic keyboard, you should consider the addition of a keyboard wrist pad.

As you can see, the position of the wrist pad reduces the stress on your wrist by elevating your hands to the keyboard height.

WHAT YOU NEED TO KNOW

All PCs come with keyboards, and now thousands of people are showing signs of stress on their wrists. In this lesson, you have learned about the advantages of upgrading to an ergonomic keyboard and why it is so easy to upgrade your keyboard.

As you work with or upgrade your computer, you will eventually encounter different error messages or system problems. To help you resolve common errors, Lesson 27 provides some basic troubleshooting techniques. Before you continue with Lesson 27, however, make sure that you understand the following key concepts:

- ✓ Keyboard upgrades are very simple—you simply turn off your computer, unplug your existing keyboard, and plug in the new keyboard.

- ✓ If you have experienced sore wrists due to long hours at the keyboard, you might want to upgrade to a new ergonomic keyboard.

- ✓ If the price of an ergonomic keyboard exceeds your budget, you should consider a keyboard wrist pad.

Lesson 27

Basic Troubleshooting Tips

Several of the lessons presented throughout this book have told you ways you can correct different PC problems. Unfortunately, you might not always know where you should look to find solutions for an error. This lesson examines several common PC problems and the steps you should take to correct them. By the time you finish this lesson you will know where to turn when you encounter common system errors.

YOUR PC DOES NOT START, AND YOU DO NOT HEAR THE PC FAN WHIR

If, when you turn on your PC's power, the PC does not start, and you do not hear the PC's fan whir, check the following:

- Make sure the PC's power plugs are plugged in correctly. If your PC has a small power light, and it comes on but the rest don't, you know, at least, that your computer is plugged in.

- Make sure the wall outlets being used are working—for example, plug a lamp into the socket.

- Verify that your surge suppresser is working correctly and that its breaker has not been tripped—for example, plug a lamp into the surge suppresser.

If all of the above is in working order, you might need to replace your PC's power supply, as discussed in Lesson 22.

Your System Displays a Message About Invalid System Settings

When your PC is not powered on, it uses a small battery-powered memory called the CMOS memory to keep track of specific settings such as your disk types, system memory, keyboard types, and so on. Like all batteries, the CMOS batteries will eventually fail. When your battery fails, your system will display an error message, similar to the following, when your system starts:

```
Invalid System Settings—Run Setup
```

This message can also appear when you add different hardware to your system unit, such as a new disk drive. Each time your system starts, its examines the available hardware, comparing it to your CMOS settings. If your hardware settings do not match your CMOS settings, your system will display the error message. Should this message appear, you need to reset your CMOS settings, as discussed in Lesson 6. If your CMOS battery has died, you will need to replace the battery, as discussed in Lesson 7.

Your System Displays the Message "Non-System disk or disk error"

This message normally occurs when you have left a nonbootable floppy disk in drive A when you start your computer. Should this error message occur, remove the floppy disk and press any key to start your system. If your floppy drive does not contain a disk, your hard disk may have become damaged. In such a case, start your system using a bootable floppy disk. Examine your hard disk to determine whether it is readable. If you can access the hard disk, turn to a book on DOS and examine the SYS command. If you cannot access the hard disk, you will very likely need to reformat the disk using the DOS FORMAT command. For more information on the FORMAT command, turn to the book, *Rescued by DOS*, Jamsa Press, 1993.

Your System Displays the Message "No such drive"

If, after you install a new hard drive, your system displays the message "No such drive" when you try to access the drive, perform these steps:

- Examine your system's CMOS settings, as discussed in Lesson 6, to ensure that the CMOS sees the drive.

- If you have not already done so, you will need to partition the hard disk, as discussed in Lesson 10.

Your System Displays the Message "Bad or missing Command Interpreter"

If your system displays the message "Bad or missing Command Interpreter," the file COMMAND.COM is missing from your disk's root directory. If this error message occurs, start your PC using a bootable floppy disk. Next, copy the file COMMAND.COM to your disk's root directory. Examine the root directory file CONFIG.SYS and examine the COMSPEC entry, which tells DOS where to locate the COMMAND.COM file. Make sure the entry points to the file's correct location on your disk. The file COMMAND.COM is responsible for displaying the DOS prompt and processing the commands you type.

Your System Displays the Message "Bad command or file name"

If, when you type in a DOS command, your screen displays the message "Bad command or file name," you might have mistyped the command. Second, the command might not reside on your disk or in the current directory path. Double-check your command spelling and ensure that you are using the correct command name. Next, ensure that the command resides in the current directory or a directory defined in the DOS command path. For more information on the DOS command path, refer to the book *Rescued by DOS*, Jamsa Press, 1993.

Your System Displays the Message "Not ready reading drive"

If your system displays the message "Not ready reading drive," you are probably trying to access a floppy drive that does not contain a disk. If this error message occurs, abort the current command or place a floppy disk into the drive and retry the command.

Your System Displays the Message "Insufficient Disk Space"

If, when you run a program, your system displays the message "Insufficient disk space," your computer's disk does not have enough empty space to hold the command's result. If this message occurs, the current command will fail. If possible, delete unnecessary files to free up sufficient disk space. Otherwise, you might consider using a command such as DBLSPACE, discussed in Lesson 32, to increase your disk capacity, or you might want to upgrade your disk, as discussed in Lesson 16.

Your System Displays the Message "Insufficient memory"

If, when you run a command, your system displays the message "Insufficient memory," you have very likely invoked too many memory-resident programs or device drivers. Most PCs today have sufficient memory for common operations. If this error message appears, turn to Lesson 33, which covers memory management, to determine ways you can better use your system memory. If Windows claims to have insufficient memory, exit Windows and restart your computer. Over time, if not restarted, errors in Windows programs will consume Windows available memory. Next, turn to Lesson 35 and ensure that you are getting the most from your Windows memory use.

Your System Displays the Message "Internal stack overflow, system halted"

If, while you are working, your system displays the message "Internal stack overflow, system halted," a device is interrupting your processor so rapidly that your processor has run out of stack space (the memory where the processor temporarily sets aside its current work). If this error message occurs, power your PC off and on. When your system starts, edit the CONFIG.SYS file and add the following entry:

```
STACKS=8,512
```

After you save the file's new contents, restart your system using the CTRL-ALT-DEL keyboard combination.

Your System Just Seems to be Running Slowly

If your system just does not seem as responsive as it used to, examine the following:

- If your system unit has a turbo switch, make sure it is on.
- Defragment your disk, as discussed in Lesson 34.

If your system performance does not improve, you might want to consider adding additional memory, as discussed in Lesson 13.

Your System Displays the Message "General failure reading (writing) drive"

If, when you try to access a drive, your system displays the message "General failure reading (writing) drive," the drive has very likely not yet been formatted. Before DOS can store information on a disk, the disk must first be formatted for use by DOS. To format a disk, you need to use the DOS FORMAT command. For more information on the DOS FORMAT command, turn to the book, *Rescued by DOS*, Jamsa Press, 1993.

Your Mouse or Modem Quits Working When You Use the Other

If, when you use your mouse, your modem stops working, or vice versa, your computer has an IRQ conflict. If such errors occur, turn to Lesson 36, which shows you how to determine IRQ use with the MSD command. Select a different IRQ setting for either your mouse or modem.

Your Mouse Does Not Respond

Not all programs support the use of a mouse. If, when you run a program, the program does not see your mouse, check the following:

- Ensure that you have installed a mouse driver—if you are using a DOS-based program, you will need to install a DOS-based device driver for the mouse (using CONFIG.SYS or AUTOEXEC.BAT).
- Ensure that the program is configured to use the mouse.
- Ensure that the mouse can be seen by a program, such as Windows, with which you have used the mouse in the past.
- Double-check your mouse cable connection to ensure that it is secure.

If none of your programs can see the mouse, ensure that the card into which the mouse connects is secure within its expansion slot. Because a mouse is a mechanical device, a mouse can fail over time. Likewise, it is also possible for a mouse cable to go bad (try wiggling the wire while moving the mouse).

YOUR MOUSE IS NOT VERY RESPONSIVE

If your mouse does not seem as responsive as it once was, you might simply need to clean the mouse. Turn to Lesson 23 and follow the steps discussed. Likewise, if you are using Windows, you can use the Control Panel to increase or decrease mouse responsiveness.

YOUR PRINTER DOES NOT PRINT

If, when you try to print, nothing happens, check the following:

- Make sure the printer is plugged in and powered on.
- Make sure the printer cable is securely connected to the printer and your PC.
- If you are using Windows, make sure Windows is configured to use the correct printer port.
- Use the MSD command to test your printer, as discussed in Lesson 36.

It is possible for a printer cable, parallel port, or printer electronics to go bad. Many printers contain their own diagnostic programs—if yours doesn't or the diagnostic shows nothing wrong, you might need to have your printer tested by your computer retailer.

YOUR PRINTER PRINTS SLOWLY

If your printer does not seem as responsive as it once did, check the following:

- If you are using Windows, examine the Print Manager's priority settings.
- Make sure you are using a parallel cable, as opposed to a serial cable.

As discussed in Lesson 25, one of the best ways to improve your system performance is to install more printer memory.

YOUR MONITOR HAS EXCESSIVE GLARE

If your monitor has excessive glare, you might be able to adjust the monitor's tilt to reduce the glare (rotate it away from the light source slightly). In addition, you might want to fine-tune the monitor's brightness and contrast. Finally, as discussed in Lesson 19, you might want to add a glare reducing screen cover.

YOUR KEYBOARD DOES NOT RESPOND

If you type and the keystrokes are ignored, double-check your keyboard cabling to ensure that the cable is securely in place. If the keystrokes are still ignored, you might need to unplug and plug in your keyboard cables. Finally, power your system off and on. In most cases, an entire keyboard will normally not fail. If you have keyboard problems, it is normally a stuck key or a single key that is ignored. Should your keyboard ignore a specific key, your keyboard very likely needs cleaning. In such cases, purchase a small aerosol blower from your computer retailer and blow out the dust that surrounds the keys.

YOUR PC SOUNDS A SERIES OF BEEPS WHEN IT STARTS

As you know, when you turn on the PC's power, your system performs a self-test of its internal components. Should the PC experience an error during the self-test, the PC may sound a series of beeps to help you determine the cause of the error. Table 27.1 lists the meanings of the self-test beeps for the commonly used Phoenix BIOS.

Beep Combinations	Meaning
1-1-3	Error accessing the CMOS memory
1-1-4	Error in the BIOS checksum (a value that double-checks settings)
1-2-1	Programmable internal timer failure
1-2-2	DMA initialization failure
1-2-3	DMA page register failure
1-3-1	RAM refresh failure
1-3-3	First 64Kb RAM failure
1-3-4	First 64Kb RAM even/odd logic failure
1-4-2	First 64Kb RAM parity error
2-*-*	First 64Kb RAM bit failure
3-1-1	Slave DMA register failure
3-1-2	Master DMA register failure
3-1-3	Master interrupt mask register failure
3-1-4	Slave interrupt mask register failure
3-2-4	Keyboard controller failure
3-3-4	Screen initialization failure
3-4-1	Screen retrace failure
4-2-1	Timer interrupt test failure
4-2-2	Shutdown test failure
4-2-3	A20 gate failure
4-2-4	Protected mode interrupt failure
4-3-1	RAM test failure above 64Kb
4-3-3	Internal timer channel 2 failure
4-3-4	Time-of-day clock failure
4-4-1	Serial port failure
4-4-2	Parallel port failure
4-4-3	Math coprocessor failure

* Asterisk indicates wildcard—it doesn't matter how many beeps in this position.

Table 27.1 The meaning of Phoenix BIOS self-test beeps.

YOUR PC DOES NOT DISPLAY VIDEO

If you turn on your PC and no video appears, check the following:

- Make sure your monitor is plugged in, powered on, and its cables are securely in place. Does the power light come on when you switch the set on?

- Make sure your monitor is securely connected to the video card.

- If necessary, unplug your system unit, remove the system unit cover, and ensure that the video card is securely in place within its expansion slot.

- If possible, test the video card by connecting a different monitor.

A WORD ON CLEANING

Ideally, you should keep your computer in a smoke- and dust-free environment. As a rule, you can keep your PC very clean simply by dusting it with a cloth. Never dust, clean, or spray a cleaner on your PC while the PC is powered on or plugged in. Also, to keep your PC clean, all you really need is a lint-free cloth, some Q-tips, a little rubbing alcohol, and an aerosol blower.

In general, if you keep your PC dust- and smoke-free, you will greatly reduce your chance of disk errors, stuck keys, and overheated PC components.

WHAT YOU NEED TO KNOW

In this lesson, you have learned how to deal with many of the more common error messages you might encounter when you work with your PC. Many of the error messages you will encounter while you work with your computer are application errors, generated by such programs as Windows, DOS, or even your word processor. When your screen displays an error message after your PC has been running for some time, turn to the documentation that accompanied the application when the error occurred.

Before continuing with Lesson 28, review the following troubleshooting tips—remembering them might save you an enormous amount of time and trouble:

- ✓ Try the easiest and least expensive fix first and work your way gradually toward the most difficult and expensive. For example, check the plug before you dismantle the power supply.

- ✓ If you change any settings, take notes on how they were before you started. If you remove or change any physical switches or parts, either take notes or a Polaroid photo. That way, you'll have the original settings fresh.

- ✓ Read the manual. You just might find your exact problem and its solution described in detail.

✓ Do one fix at a time. If your fix doesn't work, put your PC back the way it was and try another fix. You can lose control of your status if you try too many things at once.

✓ Think functionally and sequentially. These things all follow basic rules of physics—although it might seem like it, there are no computer gremlins. If you think about the order of the process, the place to locate the problem might become apparent.

✓ Ask user groups or tech support. Sometimes an apparently catastrophic error is common or has a common fix.

Section Four

SOFTWARE UPGRADES

Software upgrades are often more subtle than hardware upgrades. While it is easy to see (or hear) a new hard drive, for example, it is more difficult to notice the doubling of your disk's storage capacity through a program such as DBLSPACE, even though you might actually get more storage space from the software upgrade. You will find that software upgrades are generally less expensive than hardware upgrades, and they have no moving parts! Software upgrades are necessary for you to take full advantage of the power of your computer—without software, hardware isn't very useful. The lessons presented in this section include the following:

Lesson 28

Understanding Device Drivers

When you install different hardware components, there may be times when you need to install special software, called a *device driver*, which must be in place before DOS or Windows can recognize and use the device. If your hardware requires a device driver, you will normally receive software on a floppy disk when you buy your device. Usually, you direct your operating system (DOS) to load device driver software into your computer's memory each time your computer starts. To direct DOS to load device driver software, you use a special file named CONFIG.SYS.

In this lesson, you will learn how to place device driver entries into the CONFIG.SYS file. By the time you finish this lesson, you will understand the following:

- A device driver is special software that lets your operating system (DOS) or Windows (and your applications) recognize and use a hardware device

- Before you can use a device, driver software must be loaded into your computer's memory

- To load device driver software using DOS, you place special entries in the CONFIG.SYS file

- After changing CONFIG.SYS, you must restart your system for the changes to take effect

- DOS provides several device drivers you may use in lessons presented throughout this book

VIEWING THE CONTENTS OF YOUR CONFIG.SYS FILE

Each time your system starts, DOS searches your disk's root directory for a special file named CONFIG.SYS. If DOS locates the file, DOS uses the entries the file contains to configure your system. If the file is not found, DOS uses its default settings. To display the contents of your CONFIG.SYS file, select the root directory using the DOS CHDIR command, as shown here:

```
C:\WINDOWS> CHDIR  \   <ENTER>
C:\>
```

Next, use the EDIT command to display your file's contents:

```
C:\> EDIT  CONFIG.SYS  <ENTER>
```

In most cases, EDIT will display a screen full of entries, similar to those shown in Figure 28.1.

```
 File  Edit  Search  Options                                  Help
                          CONFIG.SYS
DEVICE=C:\DOS\SETVER.EXE
DEVICE=C:\DOS\HIMEM.SYS /M:1
DEVICE=C:\DOS\EMM386.EXE RAM X=C600-C6FF
DEVICEHIGH=C:\DOS\DBLSPACE.SYS /MOVE
devicehigh=c:\doublecd\mvsound.sys d:5 q:7 s:1,220,1,5 m:0 j:1
devicehigh=c:\doublecd\tslcdr.sys /d:mvcd001 /w3
FILES=30
BUFFERS=17
DOS=HIGH,UMB
LASTDRIVE=H
FCBS=4,0
SHELL=C:\DOS\COMMAND.COM C:\DOS\ /E:1024 /p
STACKS=9,256




MS-DOS Editor  <F1=Help> Press ALT to activate menus         N 00001:001
```

Figure 28.1 Viewing CONFIG.SYS entries with EDIT.

Note: If your system does not have a CONFIG.SYS file, create one now using EDIT. In this case, place the following two entries within the file:

```
FILES=20
BUFFERS=30
```

*Next, turn to the book **Rescued by DOS**, Jamsa Press, 1993, to learn more about the CONFIG.SYS entries. Restart your computer for the CONFIG.SYS changes to take effect.*

If your system has a CONFIG.SYS file, use the Print option on EDIT's File menu to print the file's contents at this time. Place the printout in a safe location. If a new entry in your CONFIG.SYS file one day keeps your system from starting, you can use this printout of the file's contents to restore working entries.

For now, leave the file's contents unchanged. Use the File menu's Exit option to exit EDIT back to the DOS prompt.

UNDERSTANDING CONFIG.SYS

Each time your system starts, DOS searches your disk's root directory for a special file named CONFIG.SYS. If the file is found, DOS uses the entries the file contains to configure itself in memory. If the file is not found, DOS uses default settings.

When you install different hardware components, there may be times when you need to load special software, called a device driver, into your computer's memory. To load the device driver, you normally place an entry in your CONFIG.SYS file. Device drivers are stored in files on disk, much like programs. Most device drivers use the SYS extension, such as MOUSE.SYS.

UNDERSTANDING CONFIG.SYS ENTRIES

When you examine your CONFIG.SYS file, you will find that CONFIG.SYS consists of several single-line entries, as shown here:

```
DEVICE=C:\DOS\HIMEM.SYS
DEVICE=C:\DOS\EMM386.EXE NOEMS
DOS=HIGH,UMB
BUFFERS=4
FILES=40
LASTDRIVE=Z
PROMPT $P$G
DEVICEHIGH=C:\DOS\ANSI.SYS
DEVICEHIGH=C:\DOS\DBLSPACE.SYS /MOVE
SHELL=C:\DOS\COMMAND.COM C:\DOS\ /p
```

Single-line CONFIG.SYS entries

For now, don't worry about each entry's purpose. Instead, keep in mind that each entry uses a single line. When DOS starts, it reads these entries to configure itself in memory.

INSTALLING A DEVICE DRIVER

In most cases, the documentation that accompanies your hardware board will include instructions that specify the steps you should perform to install the corresponding device driver. To begin, you will normally edit your CONFIG.SYS file and place a DEVICE (or DEVICEHIGH) entry within the file. Assume, for example, that you want to install the ANSI.SYS device driver file, which resides in the DOS directory. To install this driver, you would place the following entry in your CONFIG.SYS file:

```
DEVICE=C:\DOS\ANSI.SYS
```

As you can see, the DEVICE entry specifies the complete directory path to the device driver file, which in this case is C:\DOS.

Note: When you edit your CONFIG.SYS file, do not use a word processor. As you know, word processors let you format text, possibly using **bold** or <u>underlined</u> or by justifying text. To perform these operations, word processors embed special hidden characters within your document. Although these characters are meaningful to your word processor, they will not be meaningful to DOS within your CONFIG.SYS file. As a result, errors will occur when DOS tries to read the file's contents. To edit your CONFIG.SYS file, use an ASCII text editor such as the EDIT command provided with DOS.

In some cases, your instructions may tell you to copy the device driver from a floppy disk to your hard disk. To simplify their instructions, some vendors will tell you to copy the file to your hard disk (usually your root directory, DOS directory, or a separate sound card driver directory). For example, assume that you are installing a new mouse. Your installation notes tell you to copy the file MOUSE.SYS from the floppy disk in drive A to the root directory of your hard disk. To do so, you would use the COPY command as follows:

```
C:\> COPY   A:MOUSE.SYS  *.*   <ENTER>
```

After the COPY command completes, you could install the device driver in your CONFIG.SYS file using the following entry:

```
DEVICE=MOUSE.SYS
```

Because the device driver resides in the hard disk's root directory, you did not need to precede the filename with a directory path.

Most users, however, like to keep their disk's root directory relatively clutter-free. Rather than copying the file to your disk's root directory, you should first create a directory to hold the driver file (or you may have a directory for drivers). In this case, for example, you might create a directory named MOUSE using the MKDIR command, as shown here:

```
C:\> MKDIR  \MOUSE  <ENTER>
```

Next, you can copy the file from the floppy disk in drive A to the directory using this COPY command:

```
C:\> COPY  A:MOUSE.SYS  C:\MOUSE\*.*   <ENTER>
```

Within your CONFIG.SYS file, you would use the following DEVICE entry to install the device driver:

```
DEVICE=C:\MOUSE\MOUSE.SYS
```

As you can see, the entry specifies the complete pathname to the file. After you place the DEVICE entry into your CONFIG.SYS file, you must restart your system for the change to take effect (make sure you've saved all work in progress and exited any running programs). To restart DOS, exit all programs and press the CTRL-ALT-DEL keyboard combination.

INSTALLING A DEVICE DRIVER

A device driver is special software that lets DOS or Windows use a hardware device. Normally, users load this special device driver software when their system starts. One way to install device driver software is using the CONFIG.SYS DEVICE entry by following these steps:

1. Copy the device driver file to your hard disk, ideally placing the file in a directory other than the root.

2. Edit your CONFIG.SYS file using an ASCII text editor such as EDIT.

3. Place a DEVICE entry within CONFIG.SYS that specifies the complete pathname to the device driver file.

4. Save your changes to the CONFIG.SYS file and exit your editor.

5. Restart your system for your changes to take effect.

UNDERSTANDING *DEVICE* VERSUS *DEVICEHIGH*

If you examine the CONFIG.SYS entries presented earlier in this lesson, you will find that some entries use the DEVICE entry, while others use DEVICEHIGH:

```
DOS=HIGH,UMB                              Using the DEVICE entry
DEVICE=C:\DOS\HIMEM.SYS
DEVICE=C:\DOS\EMM386.EXE NOEMS
BUFFERS=4
FILES=40                                  Using the DEVICEHIGH entry
DEVICEHIGH=C:\DOS\ANSI.SYS
DEVICEHIGH=C:\DOS\DBLSPACE.SYS /MOVE
SHELL=C:\DOS\COMMAND.COM C:\DOS\  /p
```

Both the DEVICE and DEVICEHIGH entries let you install a device driver. The difference between the two entries is the location in memory DOS uses to install the driver. Lesson 33 discusses DOS memory management. At that time, you will learn that the DEVICEHIGH entry lets you install a device driver into the upper memory area, which is normally reserved. By installing device drivers into this area, you can free up memory for use by your DOS-based

based programs. Before you can use the DEVICEHIGH entry, you must configure DOS to support the upper-memory area. For more information on memory management, turn to Lesson 33 or the book *Rescued by DOS*, Jamsa Press, 1993.

INSTALLING A DEVICE DRIVER WITH *AUTOEXEC.BAT*

Most of the device drivers you will install will use DEVICE entries within the CONFIG.SYS file, as just discussed. In some cases, however, a device driver is installed using a DOS command. In such cases, you will install the device driver command (or the installation program might do this for you automatically) within the special batch file named AUTOEXEC.BAT.

Like the CONFIG.SYS file, AUTOEXEC.BAT resides in your disk's root directory. Using the following TYPE command, you can display the file's contents:

```
C:\> TYPE  AUTOEXEC.BAT  <ENTER>
```

To place an entry within the AUTOEXEC.BAT file, you can use the EDIT command as previously discussed. You can also use EDIT to print a copy of the file's contents. Prior to each change you make to the AUTOEXEC.BAT file (or each software installation), you should print a copy of the file's contents. In this way, should your system fail to start following the installation, you can quickly determine the new entries within the file.

UNDERSTANDING THE *AUTOEXEC.BAT* FILE

Each time your system starts, DOS searches your disk's root directory for a special batch file named AUTOEXEC.BAT, which contains a list of commands you want DOS to automatically (AUTO) execute (EXEC). Commands commonly found in AUTOEXEC.BAT include the PROMPT command, which defines your system prompt; the PATH command, which tells DOS where to locate your program files (within which directories); and device driver entries.

For more specifics on AUTOEXEC.BAT and its uses, refer to the book *Rescued by DOS*, Jamsa Press, 1993.

RECOVERING FROM A *CONFIG.SYS* OR *AUTOEXEC.BAT* ERROR

When you add a device driver entry to your CONFIG.SYS or AUTOEXEC.BAT files, there may be times when the driver does not work. Unfortunately, because DOS loads the driver before it displays your system prompt, an errant device driver can sometimes prevent your system from starting. Should you encounter a device driver error that prevents your system from starting, you will need to start without loading the device driver so you can edit the corresponding file to correct or remove the device driver entry.

If you are using a version of DOS previous to DOS 6, you will need to reboot with a dependable boot floppy (to learn how to make one, refer to the book *Rescued by DOS*, Jamsa Press, 1993) and then edit your CONFIG.SYS or AUTOEXEC.BAT.

If you are using DOS 6 or later, you can direct DOS to alter its normal system startup operations by pressing the **F5** or **F8** function keys immediately after DOS displays the following message on your screen display:

```
Starting MS-DOS . . .
```

If, when this message appears, you press the **F5** function key, DOS will bypass the CONFIG.SYS and AUTOEXEC.BAT processing, displaying instead, the DOS prompt.

When you bypass CONFIG.SYS and AUTOEXEC.BAT processing by pressing **F5**, DOS will start a minimal system. You will not have a complete command path defined. Likewise, you cannot open more than three files at any given time. Bypassing the system startup in this way provides you with an opportunity to correct errors within CONFIG.SYS or AUTOEXEC.BAT.

Assume, for example, that an entry in your CONFIG.SYS file is causing an error that hangs your system. To correct the error, restart your system. When DOS displays its starting message, press the **F5** function key. DOS will start, displaying its DOS prompt. Next, use the following command to edit the contents of your CONFIG.SYS file:

```
C:\> \DOS\EDIT  CONFIG.SYS  <ENTER>
```

You should note that the command includes a complete pathname for the DOS EDIT command. When you bypass CONFIG.SYS and AUTOEXEC.BAT processing, you bypass your PATH command (in AUTOEXEC.BAT), which establishes a command path. As such, if use an editor other than EDIT, you will need to first change to the directory that contains the editor or you must specify a complete pathname. After you correct the CONFIG.SYS entry, restart your system using the **CTRL-ALT-DEL** keyboard combination.

Note: When you bypass your CONFIG.SYS and AUTOEXEC.BAT files using the F5 function key, DOS will set your command prompt to display the current drive and directory. Your default PATH will be set to the directory that contains your DOS command files (normally C:\DOS).

BYPASSING CONFIG.SYS AND AUTOEXEC.BAT

If you find that an entry in your CONFIG.SYS or AUTOEXEC.BAT is causing an error that prevents your system from starting, you can direct DOS 6 and later to bypass its processing of these files. (Earlier versions of DOS must be started by a boot floppy) To bypass CONFIG.SYS and AUTOEXEC.BAT, press the **F5** function key when DOS displays the following message:

```
Starting MS-DOS...
```

DOS will start a minimal system from which you can change CONFIG.SYS or AUTOEXEC.BAT as required. After you make your changes, you can restart your system using the **CTRL-ALT-DEL** keyboard combination.

PROCESSING SPECIFIC CONFIG.SYS AND AUTOEXEC.BAT ENTRIES

As you just learned, pressing the **F5** function key when your system starts directs DOS 6 and later to not process CONFIG.SYS and AUTOEXEC.BAT. In a similar way (in DOS 6 and later), by pressing the **F8** function key when your system starts, you can select specific CONFIG.SYS and AUTOEXEC.BAT entries for processing. For example, assume that your CONFIG.SYS file contains the following entries:

```
FILES=20
BUFFERS=30
DEVICE=C:\DOS\HIMEM.SYS
```

If, when your system starts, you press the **F8** function key, DOS will display a prompt for each entry, asking you if you want to process the entry as shown here:

```
FILES=20 [Y,N]?
```

If you press **Y**, DOS will process the FILES entry. If you instead press **N**, DOS will ignore the entry, just as if the entry were not in the file. Next, DOS will display a similar prompt for the BUFFERS entry:

```
BUFFERS=30 [Y,N]?
```

DOS will perform this processing for each entry in the CONFIG.SYS file. Next, DOS will display the following message asking you if you want to process the AUTOEXEC.BAT entries:

```
Process AUTOEXEC.BAT [Y,N]?
```

If you press **Y**, DOS will display a prompt for each command in the AUTOEXEC.BAT file, letting you select the commands you want to execute. If you instead press **N**, DOS will not process any of the commands in the AUTOEXEC.BAT file.

CONTROLLING *CONFIG.SYS* AND *AUTOEXEC.BAT* PROCESSING

Depending on your CONFIG.SYS or AUTOEXEC.BAT entries, there may be times when you want DOS 6 or later not to process only specific entries. To perform such processing, press the **F8** function key when your system starts. DOS, in turn, will prompt you for each entry in your CONFIG.SYS and AUTOEXEC.BAT files, for example:

```
FILES=20 [Y,N]?
```

If you press **Y**, DOS will process the entry or command. If you instead press **N**, DOS will bypass the entry.

WHAT YOU NEED TO KNOW

Many hardware devices require you to install device driver software so that DOS and Windows can recognize and use the hardware device. In this lesson, you have learned how to install device drivers for DOS and how to fix errors in your CONFIG.SYS and AUTOEXEC.BAT files.

If you use Microsoft Windows, there will be times when you will need to tell Windows about new hardware. In Lesson 29, you will examine the steps you must perform to notify Windows of your hardware. Before you continue with Lesson 29, make sure you have learned the following:

✓ A device driver is a special software program that lets your computer use a specific piece of hardware. When you install a new card within your computer, such as a scanner or mouse, you will need to install device driver software before your computer can use the device.

✓ To install device driver software, you either place an entry within the CONFIG.SYS file or a command within the special batch file AUTOEXEC.BAT. In many cases, the installation program that accompanies your card will perform these operations for you.

✓ If you make a change to your CONFIG.SYS or AUTOEXEC.BAT file that causes an error that prevents your system from starting, you can press the **F5** function key when you first start your system to direct DOS 6 or later to ignore CONFIG.SYS and AUTOEXEC.BAT. Earlier versions of DOS require you to reboot from a boot floppy.

✓ If you use the **F5** function key to bypass CONFIG.SYS and AUTOEXEC.BAT, DOS 6 or later will start a minimal system. From the DOS prompt, use the EDIT command (specify a complete pathname to invoke EDIT) to make your changes to CONFIG.SYS or AUTOEXEC.BAT. When you have finished, press the CTRL-ALT-DEL keyboard combination to restart your system.

✓ In some cases, you might want DOS 6 or later to process only specific CONFIG.SYS and AUTOEXEC.BAT entries. To do so, press the **F8** function key as your system starts. DOS, in turn, will display a prompt for each CONFIG.SYS and AUTOEXEC.BAT entry. To process the entry, press **Y**. To bypass the entry, press **N**.

Lesson 29

Telling Windows About Your Hardware Upgrade

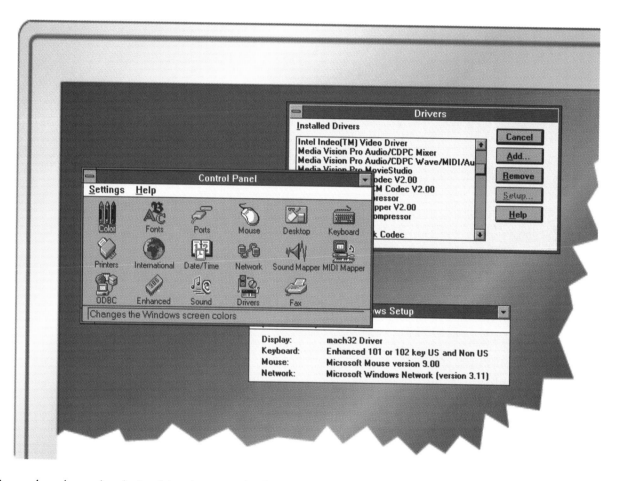

As you have learned, a device driver is a special software program that lets your PC use a hardware device. In Lesson 28 you learned how to install DOS device drivers. If you use Windows, there will be times when you will need to tell Windows about your hardware upgrade. This lesson examines the steps you must perform to notify Windows of a hardware upgrade. By the time you finish this lesson, you will understand the following key concepts:

- How to use the Setup program to inform Windows of a change to your video, keyboard, mouse, or network

- How to use the Control Panel Drivers icon to install device drivers for use with a sound card or video player

This lesson examines a few key concepts that let you tell Windows about your hardware. If you make extensive use of Windows, there are several ways you can improve Windows' performance. For specifics on fine-tuning Windows, turn to the book *Jamsa's 1001 Windows Tips*, Jamsa Press, 1993.

USING THE WINDOWS SETUP COMMAND

If you have upgraded your video card, keyboard, or mouse, or added a network, you inform Windows of the change using the Setup program. As Figure 29.1 shows, the Setup program icon resides within the Program Manager's Main window.

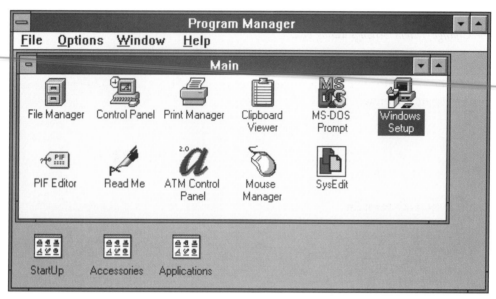

Figure 29.1 *The Setup icon resides in the Program Manager's Main window.*

When you double-click your mouse on the Setup icon, Windows will display the Windows Setup dialog box, as shown in Figure 29.2.

Figure 29.2 *The Windows Setup dialog box.*

The Setup dialog box displays your current display, keyboard, mouse, and network settings. To change a setting, select the Options menu and choose the Change System Settings option. Windows, in turn, will display the Change System Settings dialog box, as shown in Figure 29.3.

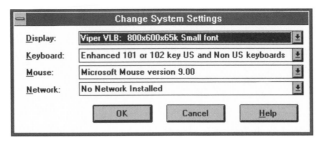

Figure 29.3 The Change System Settings dialog box.

The Change System Settings dialog box presents four pull-down lists. To display a pull-down list of setting options, click your mouse on the down arrow:

Windows will display the pull-down list:

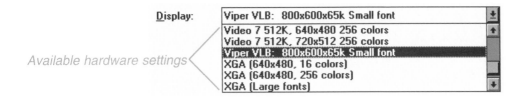

Using your keyboard arrow keys or by clicking your mouse on the scroll bar, you can scroll through the available options. If you find the option that matches your new hardware, highlight the option and click on the OK button.

Depending on the maker of the hardware board you installed, there may be times when you cannot find a matching item within the options list. In such cases, you will need to install a software driver provided on floppy disk by your hardware manufacturer. To do so, scroll through the list of options until you encounter the option that requires a floppy from the OEM:

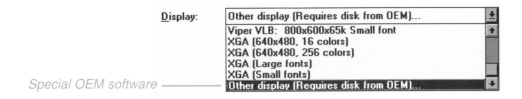

When you select this option, Windows will display the Windows Setup dialog box shown in Figure 29.4, which prompts you to insert the floppy in drive A.

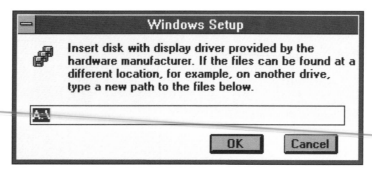

Figure 29.4 *The Windows Setup dialog box prompting for a floppy.*

Insert the disk that contains the driver and select OK. Windows, in turn, will load the corresponding device driver.

Note: *If the disks you received from the manufacturer are not labeled, search each disk's directory for a file named OEMSETUP.INF. The file contains the information Windows needs to install the driver.*

USING THE CONTROL PANEL'S DRIVERS PROGRAM

If you install a sound card, you will need to use the Control Panel Drivers icon, shown in Figure 29.5.

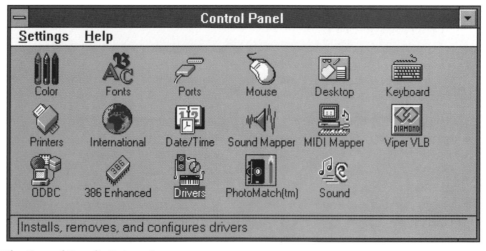

Figure 29.5 *The Control Panel's Drivers icon.*

When you double-click your mouse on the Drivers icon, Windows will display the Drivers dialog box, as shown in Figure 29.6.

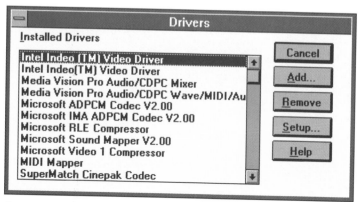

Figure 29.6 The Drivers dialog box.

The Drivers dialog box lists the sound and video player drivers currently installed on your system. To add a new driver, select the Add button. Windows will display the Add dialog box, shown in Figure 29.7.

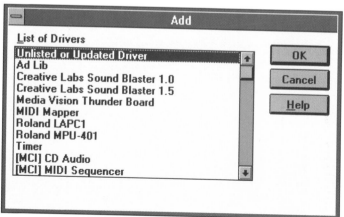

Figure 29.7 The Add dialog box.

If an option matches your new hardware, highlight the option and choose OK. Windows may then display a dialog box that prompts you to insert one of your Windows floppy disks. Insert the correct floppy and press ENTER. If you do not find a matching device, select the Unlisted or Updated Driver option. Windows will display a dialog box prompting you to insert the floppy disk that accompanied your hardware into drive A. Insert the disk and press ENTER.

WHAT YOU NEED TO KNOW

In many cases, you must inform Windows about new hardware or a hardware change. In this lesson, you have learned how to inform Windows of your hardware changes using the Windows Setup and Control Panel programs.

Much of this book's discussion has focused on installing new hardware components. As it turns out, many users have a more difficult time installing new software programs. Lesson 30 examines the steps that are common to most software installations. Before you continue with Lesson 30, however, make sure that you understand the following key concepts:

✓ When you install new hardware, there may be times when you need to inform Windows.

✓ Using the Windows Setup program, you can inform Windows of a change to your video, keyboard, mouse, or network.

✓ To install a device driver for a sound card or video player, you use the Control Panel's Drivers icon.

Lesson 30

Installing New Software

By reading this book, you have taken a big step and have begun performing your own hardware upgrades. As you have learned so far, upgrade operations are actually quite easy. Equally as important is your ability to install your own software. As you will find, software installations are normally very straightforward. Once you get one or two software installations under your belt, you'll be well on your way.

This lesson examines the steps you should perform to install software on your disk. By the time you finish this lesson, you will understand the following key concepts:

- You cannot break your computer by installing software

- You should always back up your disk before performing a major software upgrade

- Most software programs use a program named SETUP or INSTALL to perform the installation

- You can often find helpful information about a program in a README file that resides on the installation disk

- Removing software from your disk is harder than installing the software

Most major programs sold today have built-in tutorials that you can run immediately after installing the software. Using this online tutorial, you can quickly get up to speed with the program on your own.

STARTING AN INSTALLATION

Before you begin a software installation it's important to understand that you cannot break your computer by installing software on to your computer's disk. In the very worst case, the software will not work, and you will need to have a more experienced user help you determine why, to help you fix the error or help you remove the software from your disk.

As a rule, don't make your first software installation a major program, such as DOS, Windows, or the word processor you need to use everyday. If you need to install such a program, have an experienced user help you.

*Note: Never install a major software program such as DOS, Windows, or an upgrade to a program you use every day without first backing up your hard disk. In this way, should an error occur, you can quickly restore your disk to its previous contents. For more information on backing up your disk, turn to the book, **Rescued by DOS**, Jamsa Press, 1993.*

Do not start a software installation without first looking through the installation instructions that accompanied your software. If you are performing your first software installation, you may find the installation a little confusing. What you are looking for is the name of the installation program. Normally, installation programs use a name such as SETUP or INSTALL. Next, depending on whether you are working from DOS or Windows, the steps you will perform to run the installation program will differ. As you perform the software installation, keep the manual by your side.

INSTALLING A PROGRAM FROM DOS

To install a DOS-based program, insert the first disk in drive A or B. To begin the installation, you normally type in the name of the installation program, preceded by the appropriate drive letter and a colon. For example, assuming the installation program is named SETUP and your installation disk resides in drive A, you would start the installation as follows:

```
C:\> A:SETUP   <ENTER>
```

Most software programs ask you to respond to one or more questions. To simplify the installation, the programs normally provide default answers. In most cases, you can simply use the default responses. After the installation program completes, you might need to restart your computer. In some cases, the installation program will do this for you automatically.

When the installation is complete, you can run the program by typing its name at the DOS prompt and pressing ENTER. The documentation that accompanied your software will specify the correct command name you should use. If, when you type the program name, DOS displays an error message instead of running the program, DOS most likely could not find the program:

```
C:\> NEWPROG   <ENTER>
Bad command or filename
```

Should this error message occur, double-check that you are using the correct command name and that you are spelling the command name correctly. Next, verify that the program resides in the current directory. If the program resides in a different directory, use the CHDIR command to select that directory. If you have problems running a program that resides in a different directory, you might want to place the program's directory name into the PATH command defined in your AUTOEXEC.BAT. For more information on the PATH command, turn to the book *Rescued by DOS*, Jamsa Press, 1993.

INSTALLING A PROGRAM FROM WINDOWS

If you are installing a Windows-based program, you should perform the software installation from within Windows. In fact, many programs force you to be running Windows. After starting Windows, select the File menu, as shown in Figure 30.1.

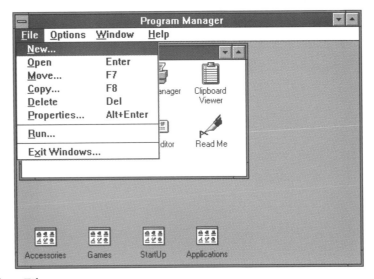

Figure 30.1 The Windows File menu.

Select the Run option. Windows will display the Run dialog box. Assuming you are running the SETUP program that resides in drive A, you would type in the program name **A:\SETUP**, as shown in Figure 30.2.

Figure 30.2 The Windows Run dialog box.

When the installation completes, you can run the program by double-clicking the program's icon. If the program provides a tutorial, take the time to run it. The time you spend within the tutorial will save you much greater time and effort in the future.

BROWSING THE README FILE

Producing software documentation is an expensive and time-consuming process. As a result, almost every software program you install provides a file on disk that contains information that did not get included in the product's documentation. Normally, the file has a name like README.TXT, READ.ME, or README.WRI. Search the first installation disk for such a file. Using your word processor, you can normally open the file and print its contents.

REMOVING A PROGRAM FROM YOUR DISK

Over time, there may be times when you want to remove a program file from your disk, normally because you no longer use the program and you now need the disk space. Unfortunately, most programs do not provide an uninstall option. To remove a program from your disk, you need working knowledge of DOS or Windows.

Note: Always back up the files on your disk before you remove a program. In this way, should you make an error or later wish you had not removed the file, you can quickly restore the files.

PROGRAMS RESIDE IN DIRECTORIES

When you install a program on your disk, the program is usually placed in its own directory. The best way to visualize a directory is as a filing cabinet drawer, within which only the files related to the program are placed. To remove a program from you disk, you remove the directory that contains the program files. Before you can delete program files you must identify the program's directory name. As a general rule, if you don't know how to determine the program's directory name, you should have a more experienced user assist you.

REMOVING A PROGRAM FROM YOUR DISK IN DOS

If you are using DOS 6 or later, removing a program's directory from your hard disk is relatively easy. To begin, use the CHDIR command to select the root directory as the current directory:

```
C:\> CHDIR  \   <ENTER>
```

Next, use the DELTREE command to remove the directory. Assuming, for example, that you are deleting a directory named SOMEPROG, you would use the following DELTREE command:

```
C:\> DELTREE  SOMEPROG  <ENTER>
```

If you are not using DOS 6 or later, removing a program from your disk can be more challenging. In fact, you will want an experienced user to assist you. To begin, use the CHDIR command to select the program's directory. In the case of the directory SOMEPROG, use CHDIR as follows:

```
C:\> CHDIR  \SOMEPROG   <ENTER>
C:\SOMEPROG>  ———————————— Prompt shows current directory is now SOMEPROG
```

Make sure that your DOS prompt now shows the name of the directory that you intend to delete. Next, use the DEL command to delete the files each directory contains:

```
C:\SOMEPROG> DEL  *.*  <ENTER>
```

The *.* (pronounced "asterisk dot asterisk" or "star dot star") in the DEL command tell DOS to delete all the files within the directory. Because an errant DEL command that uses *.* can have devastating results, DEL will ask you to verify the operation by displaying the following prompt:

```
All files in directory will be deleted!
Are you sure (Y/N)?
```

If you are sure that the directory is correct, press **Y** to delete the files. Next, use the DIR command to display the directories contents:

```
C:\SOMEPROG> DIR   <ENTER>
```

If you have successfully deleted all the files the directory contains, your directory listing will appear as follows:

```
C:\SOMEPROG> DIR   <ENTER>

 Volume in drive C has no label
 Volume Serial Number is 1DD2-2667
 Directory of C:\SOMEPROG

 .            <DIR>        05-22-94    3:57p
 ..           <DIR>        05-22-94    3:57p
        2 file(s)              0 bytes
                    87,949,312 bytes free
```

The two entries (. and ..) that appear in the directory listing appear in all subdirectories whether the subdirectory contains other files or not. If your directory listing only displays these two entries, the directory is empty.

Once the directory is empty, use the CHDIR command with two dots (..) to move up one level in the directory tree:

```
C:\SOMEPROG> CHDIR ..   <ENTER>
```

Next, use the RMDIR command to remove the directory:

```
C:\> RMDIR  SOMEPROG   <ENTER>
```

To improve their own file organization, many programs will use additional levels of directories. When you perform a directory listing for such a program, your directory listing will reveal additional entries such as those shown here:

```
C:\SOMEPROG> DIR   <ENTER>

 Volume in drive C has no label
 Volume Serial Number is 1DD2-2667
 Directory of C:\SOMEPROG

 .            <DIR>        05-22-94    3:57p
 ..           <DIR>        05-22-94    3:57p
 PROGRAMS     <DIR>        05-22-94    3:57p
 DATA         <DIR>        05-22-94    3:57p
        4 file(s)              0 bytes
                    87,916,544 bytes free
```

In such cases, you must perform the following steps for each directory listed (as well as lower-level directories contained within each directory):

1. Select the directory using the CHDIR command.

2. Use the DEL command to delete the directory's files.

3. Use the DIR command to display the directory's contents.

4. If the directory is empty, move up one level using the CHDIR command and then use the RMDIR command to remove the directory.

5. If the directory contains additional subdirectories, perform steps 1 through 5 for each subdirectory.

REMOVING A PROGRAM FROM WITHIN WINDOWS

Removing a program from within Windows is a two-step process. To begin, you delete the program icon from within the Program Manager. Second, you must delete the program files and directories from within the File Manager.

DELETING THE PROGRAM ICONS

To delete a program or group icon, single-click (do not double-click) your mouse on the icon to select the icon. Next, press the DEL key. Windows will display a Delete dialog box, similar to that shown in Figure 30.3, asking you to verify that you want to delete the icon. When the dialog box appears, click your mouse on the Yes option to delete the icon.

Figure 30.3 *The Delete dialog box.*

Note: *To delete a program group icon (a program group is a window that holds several program icons), minimize the group window to an icon, highlight the icon, and press DEL.*

REMOVING THE PROGRAM DIRECTORY AND FILES

To delete a program directory from within Windows, run the File Manager, as shown in Figure 30.4.

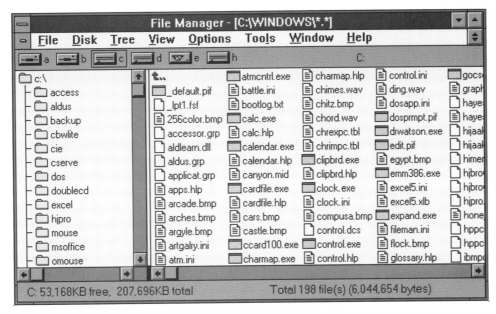

Figure 30.4 *The Windows File Manager.*

Within the File Manager directory tree, single-click (do not double-click) your mouse on the program's directory. Next, press the DEL key. Windows will display a Delete dialog box similar to that shown in Figure 30.5.

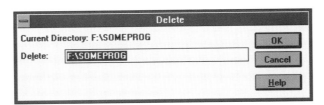

Figure 30.5 *The Delete dialog box.*

Select the OK option. Windows, in turn, will display the Confirm Directory Delete dialog box shown in Figure 30.6. Select the Yes to All button. When the delete operation completes, use the File menu to exit the File Manager.

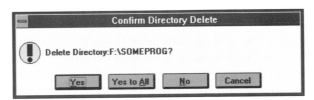

Figure 30.6 *The Confirm Directory Delete dialog box.*

WHAT YOU NEED TO KNOW

With software changing and being improved so frequently, it is important to know how to upgrade your computer's software. In this lesson, you have learned how to install and remove software from within both DOS and Windows.

One of the easiest ways to improve your system's performance is to install special software called a disk cache, which speeds up many disk operations. Lesson 31 examines the steps you must perform to install a disk cache. Before you continue with Lesson 31, however, make sure that you have learned the following key concepts:

✓ You cannot break your computer by installing software. In the worst case, the software will not work, and you must simply remove the software from your disk.

✓ You should always back up your hard disk before performing a major software upgrade. In this way, should the installation fail, you can quickly restore your disk to its previous working condition.

✓ Most software programs use a program named SETUP or INSTALL to perform the installation. The documentation that accompanied your software will specify the commands you should run to install the software.

✓ In many cases, the latest documentation about a program does not make it into the printed manual. Most software developers, therefore, will include additional information about the product on disk. You can often find help text about a program in a README file that resides on the installation disk.

✓ Removing software from your disk is harder than installing the software. The first time you remove software from your disk, you will want an experienced user to assist you. Make sure you back up the software you are removing before you remove it.

Lesson 31

Improving Disk Performance with a Disk Cache

As you have learned, disks are mechanical devices, which makes them much slower than their electronic counterparts. One of the best ways to improve your system performance is to reduce the number of slow disk read and write operations your system must perform. In this lesson you will learn how to set aside part of your computer's fast random access memory (RAM) as a disk cache, which in turn, reduces disk operations. By the time you finish this lesson, you will understand the following key concepts:

- Programs read information from disk into your computer's memory

- Programs record information from memory to disk

- A disk cache is a large memory buffer that can reduce slow disk operations

- You can create a disk cache using the SMARTDRV command provided with DOS

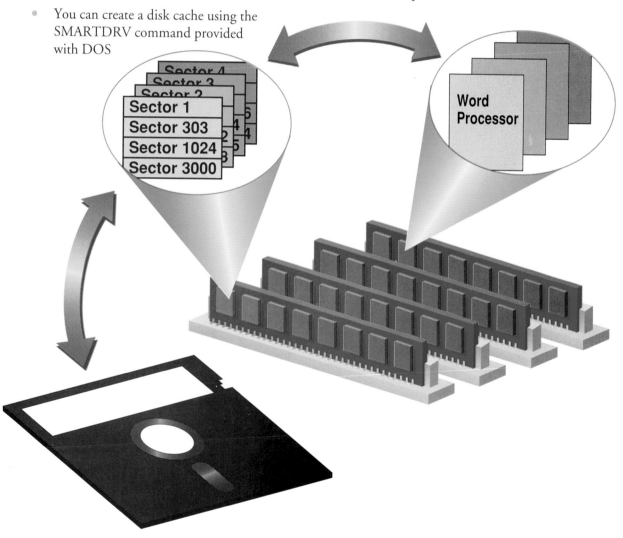

HOW PROGRAMS READ DISK INFORMATION

As you know, files let you store information from one computer session to the next.

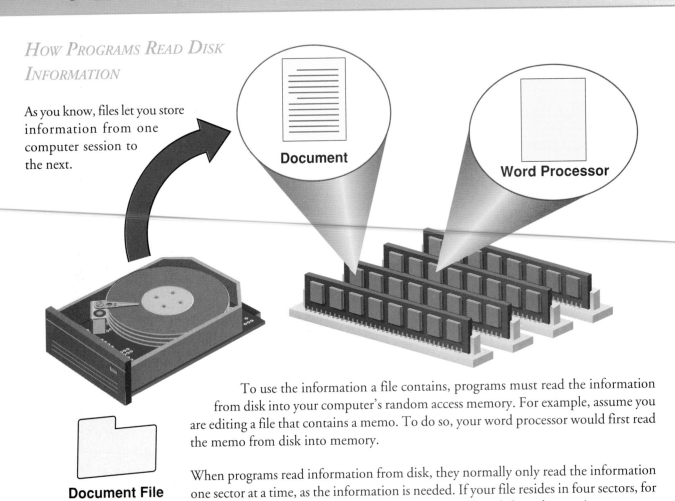

Document

Word Processor

Document File

To use the information a file contains, programs must read the information from disk into your computer's random access memory. For example, assume you are editing a file that contains a memo. To do so, your word processor would first read the memo from disk into memory.

When programs read information from disk, they normally only read the information one sector at a time, as the information is needed. If your file resides in four sectors, for example, your word processor might perform four slow disk read operations.

PROGRAMS READ INFORMATION INTO MEMORY

Before your programs can use information stored on disk, your programs must read the information into your computer's random access memory. Disks store information in storage locations called *sectors*. Programs perform disk read operations a disk sector at a time.

Because disks are mechanical devices, they are much slower than their electronic counterparts. Thus, one way to improve your system performance is to reduce the number of slow disk I/O operations your system must perform. A disk cache provides an easy way to reduce disk I/O operations.

UNDERSTANDING A DISK CACHE

A *cache* is simply a storage location. Before winter, for example, squirrels store their nuts in a cache. A *disk cache* is simply a storage location in your computer's random access memory into which disk sectors are read and stored.

As you have learned, files are stored on disk within sectors. Normally, programs will read data into memory one sector at a time—a slow process.

When you use a disk cache, extra sectors are normally read into the cache during a read operation. When a program needs information stored in subsequent sectors, the program might very likely find the information within the disk cache.

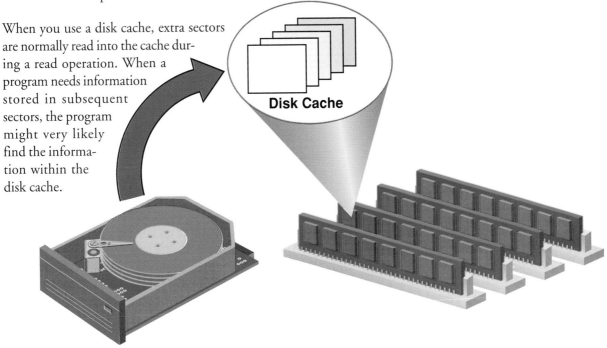

As a result, the program can quickly access the data from the computer's fast memory, eliminating the need for the slow disk read operation.

Some programs, such as a database, may reread the same information from disk. In many cases, such programs will find the data they need within the disk cache.

As a result, the programs eliminate slow disk read operations. If the desired information is not found within the cache, the information is simply read from disk.

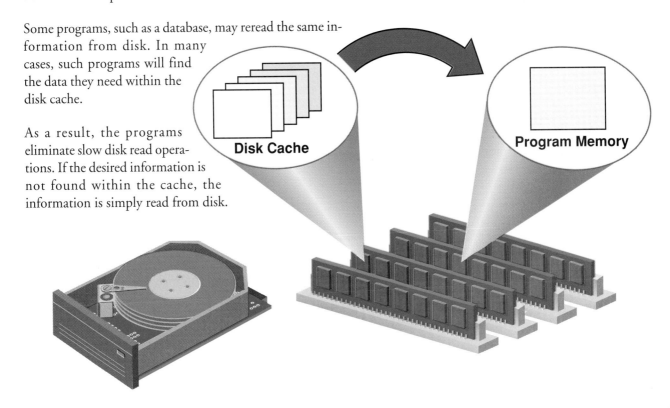

INSTALLING A DISK CACHE

A disk cache is created by a special software program. Several third-party software companies offer disk caching software. However, the most commonly used caching software is the SMARTDRV program provided free with DOS. To use SMARTDRV, your computer must contain extended memory (see Lesson 33). Most users place the SMARTDRV command in their AUTOEXEC.BAT file (see Appendix A) to ensure that the SMARTDRV disk cache is used each time their systems start.

When you use SMARTDRV, you consume extended memory to hold the disk buffer. When you use Windows, there may be times when your PC's extended memory can be put to better use than for a disk cache. As such, SMARTDRV uses two buffer sizes—one buffer size specifies the initial cache size and the second specifies the minimum size to which Windows can reduce the cache, in order to use memory better.

Depending on how much extended memory your system contains, the size of the SMARTDRV cache will differ. Table 31.1 lists the default cache sizes for different extended memory amounts.

Extended Memory	Initial Cache Size	Minimum Cache Size
1Mb	All	0Kb
2Mb	1Mb	256Kb
4Mb	1Mb	512Kb
6Mb	2Mb	1Mb
>6Mb	2Mb	2Mb

Table 31.1 Default SMARTDRV disk cache sizes.

In most cases, you can use SMARTDRV's default settings. However, when you invoke SMARTDRV, you can specify different buffer sizes. For more information on SMARTDRV settings, invoke the SMARTDRV command from the DOS prompt using the question mark switch (/?), or turn to the book *Rescued by DOS*, Jamsa Press, 1993.

```
C:\> SMARTDRV /?    <ENTER>

Installs and configures the SMARTDrive disk-caching utility.

smartdrv [[/E:elementsize] [/B:buffersize] [drive [+]|[-]] [size] [winsize]]...

drive letter      Specifies the letter of the disk drive to cache.
                  (drive letter alone specifies read caching only)
+                 Enables write-behind caching for the specified drive.
-                 Disables all caching for the specified drive.
size              Specifies the amount of XMS memory (KB) used by the cache.
winsize           Specifies the amount of XMS memory (KB) used in Windows.
/E:element size   Specifies the size of the cache elements (in bytes).
/B:buffer size    Specifies the size of the read buffer.
/C                Writes all write-behind information to the hard disk.
/R                Clears the contents of existing cache and restarts SMARTDrive.
/L                Loads SMARTDrive into low memory.
/Q                Prevents the display of SMARTDrive information on your screen.
/S                Displays additional information about the status of SMARTDrive.
```

If Windows Won't Run

If, after you install a SMARTDRV disk cache, Windows won't run, you may need to use SMARTDRV's double-buffering capabilities. As it turns out, some disk controllers (the electronics that operate the disk drive) will not work with SMARTDRV when Windows runs in 386 Enhanced mode. In such cases, you simply need to install the SMARTDRV.EXE device driver within your CONFIG.SYS file (see Appendix A) using the /DOUBLE_BUFFER switch, as shown here:

```
DEVICE=C:\DOS\SMARTDRV.EXE   /DOUBLE_BUFFER
```

You only need to use the /DOUBLE_BUFFER switch when Windows does not run after you install SMARTDRV. Normally, such errors occur when you are using the EMM386 memory manager.

*Note: When you place a device entry in your CONFIG.SYS file for SMARTDRV, you still invoke the SMARTDRV command from within AUTOEXEC.BAT. In other words, the CONFIG.SYS device driver entry is used **in addition to** the SMARTDRV command, not instead of it.*

Be Aware of Write-Behind Caching

In addition to performing caching for read operations, caching can also be used for disk write operations. When write caching is used, the information your programs write to disk is also placed into the cache. In this way, should the program need to read the information a second time, it will find the latest information contained within the cache.

To improve your system performance, write caching employs a technique called *write-behind caching*. Using this technique, the information a program writes to disk is first written to the cache and not to the disk. In this way, the program can continue without having to wait for the slow disk operation to complete. Later, after a few second delay, the information is written to disk.

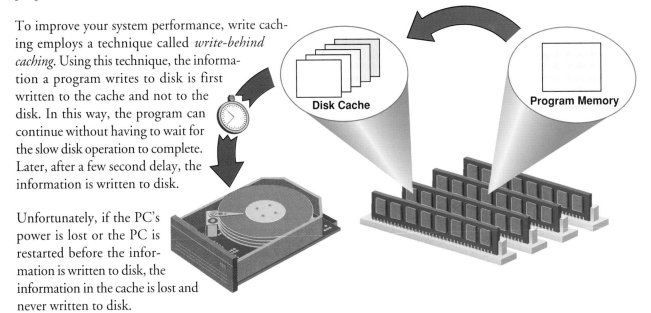

Unfortunately, if the PC's power is lost or the PC is restarted before the information is written to disk, the information in the cache is lost and never written to disk.

To eliminate this window of possible data loss, many users will disable write caching, trading increased data security for a loss of performance. To disable write-behind caching, use the following SMARTDRV command:

```
SMARTDRV  /X
```

To determine if your system is using write caching, invoke SMARTDRV from the DOS prompt as shown here:

```
C:\> SMARTDRV  <ENTER>
Microsoft SMARTDrive Disk Cache version 5.0
Copyright 1991,1993 Microsoft Corp.

Cache size:  2,097,152 bytes
Cache size while running Windows:  2,097,152 bytes

           Disk Caching Status
drive    read cache    write cache    buffering

  A:         yes            no            no
  B:         yes            no            no
  C:         yes            no            no

For help, type "Smartdrv /?".
```

Write-behind caching disabled

When you use write caching, you maximize your system performance. However, you also expose yourself to possible data loss. If you can't afford possible data loss, disable write caching.

If you are using write caching, you can get SMARTDRV to *flush* (write) all of the information in the buffer to disk immediately by using the /C switch, as follows:

```
C:\> SMARTDRV  /C  <ENTER>
```

WHAT YOU NEED TO KNOW

A disk drive, even a hard drive, is slow compared with the computer's fast electronic memory. In this chapter you have learned how to install and use a disk cache to speed up your disk operations.

No matter how you use your computer, if you are like most users, you must constantly search for ways to find available space on your disk. In Lesson 32 you will learn how you can double your disk's storage capacity using disk compression software. If you are using DOS, you may already have all the software you need. Before you continue with Lesson 32, however, make sure that you have learned the following key concepts:

- ✓ The SMARTDRV command, provided with DOS and Windows lets you create a disk cache.

- ✓ A disk cache is a large buffer in your computer's random access memory into which sectors read from your disk can be stored.

- ✓ Before DOS reads the disk for a specific sector (a slow operation), DOS first checks to see if the sector resides in the cache (a fast operation). If the sector is in the cache, DOS can quickly retrieve and use the sector.

- ✓ To prevent possible data loss when using a cache, you should disable write-behind caching by invoking SMARTDRV with the /X switch.

- ✓ If you are using write-behind caching, you can immediately write the contents of the buffer to disk by invoking SMARTDRV with the /C switch.

Lesson 32

Doubling Your Disk's Storage Capacity

No matter how they use their computers, most users can quickly consume their hard disk's available disk space. As the price of hard disks continues to drop, many users now replace their hard disks with larger ones, or possibly even add a second hard disk. Unfortunately, as fast as users add disk space, they are able to use it up. As it turns out, one of the most cost-effective ways to increase your available disk space is not by purchasing a new hard disk, but rather, to use software to double your existing disk's storage capacity.

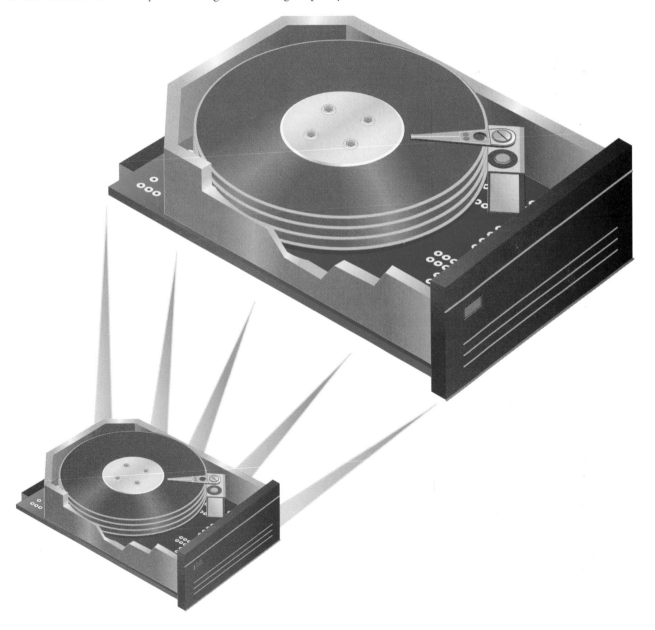

This lesson examines how you can use the DBLSPACE command provided with DOS to double your disk's storage capacity. DBLSPACE is not the only software program you can use to increase your disk's capacity. In fact, many users prefer to use a third-party software program named STACKER. This lesson, however, focuses on DBLSPACE, because many users already have it. By the time you finish this lesson, you will understand the following key concepts:

- How disk compression software doubles your disk storage capacity
- How you can double your disk storage capacity using the DBLSPACE command

What You'll Need

Before you get started on this lesson, make sure that you have the following readily available:

1. Software to back up your disk's current contents
2. Sufficient floppy disks (or other media, such as tape backup or removable drive cartridges) to store the backup
3. Disk compression software such as DBLSPACE

Understanding Disk Compression

As you know, the PC works in terms of 1s and 0s, binary digits. When your disk records information, the disk too, represents data using 1s and 0s. If you were to examine these 1s and 0s on disk, you would find many long strings of all 1s or all 0s.

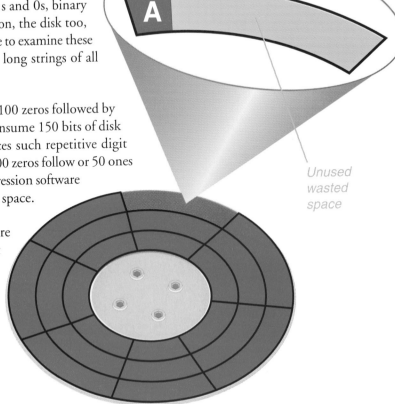

Unused wasted space

Assume, for example, that a file contains 100 zeros followed by 50 ones. These values would normally consume 150 bits of disk space. Disk compression software replaces such repetitive digit strings with a small code that states that 100 zeros follow or 50 ones follow. Using these compact codes, compression software can recover tremendous amounts of disk space.

As you have learned, disks normally store files in one or more sectors. The smallest amount of disk a file can consume is a disk sector. Even a file that contains only a single character (one byte) still consumes a disk sector. In the case of a 512 byte sector, 511 bytes would be wasted for the one-byte file.

UNDERSTANDING EXPANDED MEMORY

When the IBM PC was first released in 1981, the PC could only support 1Mb of memory. If you placed more than 1Mb of memory into your computer, the 8088 processor simply could not use it. The PC could not address (access) memory locations whose addresses were above 1Mb. Unfortunately, spreadsheet programs such as Lotus 1-2-3 quickly consumed the PC's available memory. To provide the PC with more memory, hardware developers came up with *expanded memory*, a way to trick the PC into using memory beyond 1Mb.

Today, however, expanded memory is rarely used. As such, we will not discuss its use here. If you need information on expanded memory, turn to your DOS documentation or the book *Rescued by DOS*, Jamsa Press, 1993.

UNDERSTANDING UPPER MEMORY

The PC reserves the top 384Kb of conventional memory for use by the video display and other hardware devices. Parts of this 384Kb region, called the *upper memory area*, are not used. As such, DOS lets you load device drivers and memory-resident programs into these unused areas (called upper memory blocks). Normally, DOS loads device drivers and memory-resident programs into the 640Kb program space. By moving these programs to the upper memory area, you free up more of the 640Kb program space for use by your programs.

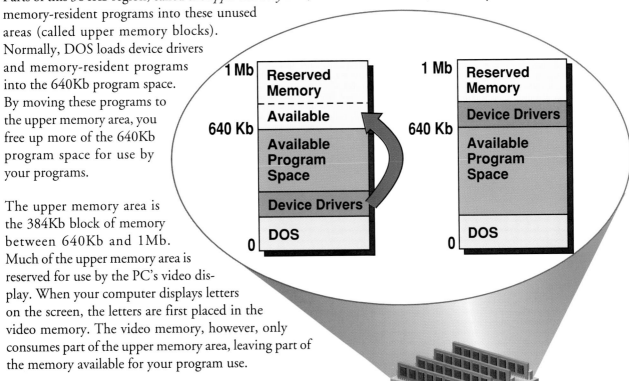

The upper memory area is the 384Kb block of memory between 640Kb and 1Mb. Much of the upper memory area is reserved for use by the PC's video display. When your computer displays letters on the screen, the letters are first placed in the video memory. The video memory, however, only consumes part of the upper memory area, leaving part of the memory available for your program use.

A *memory-resident* program is a program that remains in your computer's memory after you run it. The DOS PRINT command, for example, remains in memory to print files while you issue other commands from the DOS prompt. Likewise, as you have learned, some device drivers, such as MOUSE.COM, remain in memory to let DOS use the driver to access a specific device. Memory-resident programs and device drivers normally reside within the 640Kb program space.

You can load memory-resident programs and device drivers into the upper memory area, freeing up more of the 640Kb region for your program use.

DIRECTING DOS TO SUPPORT THE UPPER MEMORY AREA

Before you can use the upper memory area, you must tell DOS to support it. To begin, place the EMM386.EXE device driver in your CONFIG.SYS file, as shown here:

```
DEVICE=C:\DOS\EMM386.EXE    NOEMS
```

The EMM386.EXE device driver lets you allocate extended memory for use as expanded memory. In this case, the NOEMS parameter tells DOS that you do not want to use expanded memory. Instead, you are simply using the device driver to provide support for the upper memory area. Next, you must place a DOS entry similar to the following in your CONFIG.SYS file:

```
DOS=HIGH,UMB
```

UMB is an abbreviation for *upper memory block*. An upper memory block is a section of memory within the upper memory area. When you load a device driver or memory-resident program into the upper memory area, DOS will allocate an upper memory block to hold the program. After you place these entries in your CONFIG.SYS file, you must restart your system for the change to take effect.

PUTTING THE UPPER MEMORY REGION TO USE

Once you provide upper memory support, you can direct DOS to load device drivers and memory-resident programs into the upper memory area. In Lesson 28 you learned that to install a device driver you place a DEVICE entry in your CONFIG.SYS file. To install a device driver into the upper memory area, use the DEVICEHIGH entry, as shown here:

```
DEVICEHIGH=C:\DOS\ANSI.SYS
```

When DOS encounters a DEVICEHIGH entry in your CONFIG.SYS file, it first tries to load the device driver into the upper memory area. If there is not enough memory in the upper memory area to hold the driver, DOS will load the driver into the 640Kb memory region just as if you had used the DEVICE entry.

You cannot use the DEVICEHIGH entry until you have installed upper memory support. Thus, you cannot use DEVICEHIGH for the HIMEM.SYS or EMM386.EXE device drivers. The following entries illustrate how you might use DEVICEHIGH within your CONFIG.SYS file:

```
DEVICE=C:\DOS\HIMEM.SYS
DEVICE=C:\DOS\EMM386.EXE    NOEMS
DOS=HIGH,UMB
DEVICEHIGH=C:\DOS\ANSI.SYS
```

You can do a similar thing with memory-resident programs. By default, when you load a memory-resident program such as PRINT, DOS will place the program in the 640Kb program area. With support for the upper memory area, however, you can use the LOADHIGH command to place such programs into the upper memory area. For example, the following LOADHIGH command directs DOS to load the PRINT command into upper memory:

```
LOADHIGH C:\DOS\PRINT
```

Note that LOADHIGH is a command, not a CONFIG.SYS entry. You might use LOADHIGH within your AUTOEXEC.BAT file. Because of its frequency of use, DOS lets you abbreviate LOADHIGH as simply LH.

WHAT YOU NEED TO KNOW

In Lesson 34, you will learn how to improve your system's performance by defragmenting your disk. Before you continue with Lesson 34, however, make sure that you have learned the following key concepts:

✓ Your computer's electronic memory (or RAM) may consist of conventional, extended, expanded, upper, and high memory.

✓ All PCs have a 1Mb conventional memory area. Conventional memory consists of two parts: a 640Kb program space that holds DOS and programs you run and 384Kb region that is reserved for your video display and other hardware devices.

✓ Extended memory is the memory beyond the PC's 1Mb conventional memory.

✓ Before DOS can use extended memory, you must place the HIMEM.SYS device driver in your CONFIG.SYS file.

✓ DOS-based program instructions must reside in your computer's conventional memory. However, many programs let their data reside in extended memory.

✓ One of the most common ways users take advantage of extended memory is to create a large disk buffer using SMARTDRV.

✓ If you are using a 286-based computer (or higher) that contains extended memory, you can load DOS into a special memory region called the high memory area. By placing DOS into the high memory area, you free up conventional memory for your program use.

✓ The original 8088-based PC, released in 1981, could only access 1Mb of memory. Expanded memory is a technique that combines hardware and software to trick the PC into using memory beyond its 1Mb limits. Expanded memory can only store program data.

✓ If you are using a 286-based PC (or higher), you should use extended memory, which is much faster than expanded memory.

✓ The upper memory area is the 384Kb region between 640Kb and 1Mb. Much of the upper memory area is reserved for use by the PC's video. However, part of the upper memory area is available for use by DOS. To use the upper memory area, you must be using a 386-based computer or higher.

✓ By placing memory-resident programs and device drivers in the upper memory area, you free up the 640Kb program area for use by your programs.

✓ Before you can use the upper memory area, you must first install the EMM386.EXE device driver and place a DOS=UMB entry in your CONFIG.SYS file.

✓ To load a device driver in the upper memory area, use the DEVICEHIGH entry. If DOS is unable to fit the device driver into the available upper memory, DOS will load the driver into the 640Kb program area.

✓ To load a memory-resident program into the upper memory area, use the LOADHIGH command. If DOS is unable to fit the command into the available upper memory, DOS will load the program into the 640Kb program area.

Lesson 34

Defragmenting Your Hard Disk

If programs start slowly when you type the program name at the DOS prompt or when you double-click on the program icon from within Windows, files on your hard disk may be fragmented. To store information, disks record information in storage locations called sectors. A file is *fragmented* when its sectors are dispersed across your disk. As you will learn in this lesson, it takes the disk drive longer to read or write fragmented files, which makes your programs load slower.

Files become fragmented as a natural result of creating, editing, and deleting files. Fortunately, there are many different software programs you can run that *defragment* your disk. If you are concerned about system performance, you should run such programs on a regular basis. This lesson presents one such program, DEFRAG, which is included with DOS 6 or later. By the time you finish this lesson, you will understand the following concepts:

- How your disk drive reads and writes files

- How fragmented files decrease your system performance

- How files become fragmented

- How to correct fragmented files

*Note: When you defragment your files, software moves the information stored on your disk. Do not use disk defragmentation software unless you have a recent backup of the files on your disk. For more information on performing system backups, turn to the book **Rescued by DOS**, Jamsa Press, 1993.*

HOW A DISK READS AND WRITES INFORMATION

To store information, your disk records information in storage locations on the disk's surface called *sectors*. As you can see, a disk contains rows of concentric circles called *tracks*. Each track is further divided into fixed-sized sectors. A disk sector typically stores 512 bytes (characters) of data.

To read or record information, the disk drive uses a read/write head, which is similar to an audio tape head that works like a needle used by old record players. Like a record album, the disk spins past the read/write head. Unlike an album that rotates very slowly, your hard disk spins very quickly, at 3,600 revolutions per minute.

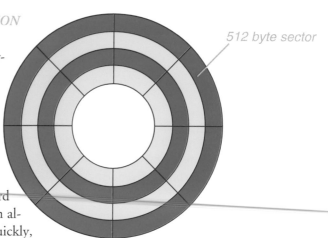

512 byte sector

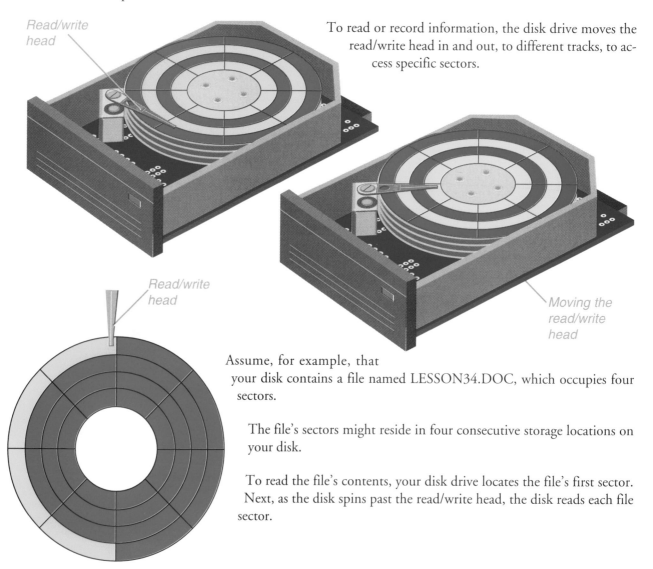

Read/write head

To read or record information, the disk drive moves the read/write head in and out, to different tracks, to access specific sectors.

Moving the read/write head

Read/write head

Assume, for example, that your disk contains a file named LESSON34.DOC, which occupies four sectors.

The file's sectors might reside in four consecutive storage locations on your disk.

To read the file's contents, your disk drive locates the file's first sector. Next, as the disk spins past the read/write head, the disk reads each file sector.

How Fragmented Files Decrease Your System Performance

As you just learned, to read a file's contents, the disk drive must read the file's sectors as they spin past the disk read/write head.

In the previous example, the file's sectors resided in consecutive sectors. Files whose sectors reside in consecutive locations are *contiguous*.

On the other hand, files whose sectors do not reside in consecutive storage locations are fragmented.

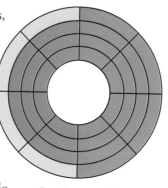

Contiguous file

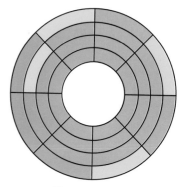

Fragmented file

Unlike your computer's fast electronic parts, such as memory or the CPU, a disk drive is a mechanical device—the disk spins within the drive and the read/write head must move in and out to access sectors that reside in different tracks. Because the disk drive is mechanical, it is much slower than its electronic counterparts. An easy way to improve system performance, is to reduce the number of slow disk operations your computer must perform.

Correcting fragmented files does just that. Assume, for example, that the file LESSON34.DOC, just discussed, resides in sectors that are dispersed across your disk.

To read the file's contents, the disk drive locates the file's first sector. After reading the first sector, the disk drive must wait (over half a revolution) for the second sector to spin past the read/write head.

Next, to read the third sector, the disk drive must first move the read/write head to the correct track, then wait for that sector to spin past the head.

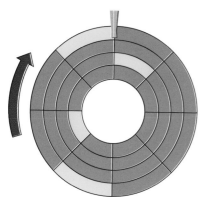

Finally, to read the last sector, the disk drive must again move the read/write head, then wait for the sector to spin past. To read the fragmented file, the disk drive had to repeatedly wait for the sector to spin past the read/write head. Such rotational delays add up, increasing the amount of time it takes to read a file, which in turn, decreases your system performance.

HOW FILES BECOME FRAGMENTED

Files become fragmented naturally as you create, edit, and delete files. You are not doing anything wrong if your disk becomes fragmented. In most cases, you can't prevent fragmented files—instead, you simply correct them. Assume, for example, that you start a letter to a friend. When you save the file to disk, the information is recorded in a disk sector.

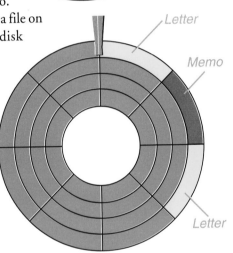

Next, assume that as you are working on the letter, you have to stop typing so you can type an office memo. When you save the memo to a file on disk, it will be stored in a disk sector.

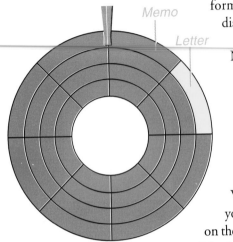

When the memo is complete, you might resume your work on the letter you previously saved to disk. As the length of your letter grows, the letter might require several disk sectors.

In this case, when the rest of the letter is recorded to disk, it is placed in a sector that is not consecutive with the previous sector. As a result, the file containing your letter is now fragmented.

RECOGNIZING THE SYMPTOMS

As you have learned, fragmented files decrease your system performance by increasing the amount of time it takes the disk drive to read the file on your disk. If, when you run a program from the DOS prompt or from within Windows, the program seems to load slowly, your disk might be fragmented. Fragmented files occur naturally, simply by creating, editing, and deleting files on your disk. You cannot prevent fragmentation; instead, you correct it when the symptoms become present.

CORRECTING FRAGMENTED FILES

To correct fragmented files, you run a special software program that moves the information your files contain, placing the information into consecutive sectors on your disk. There are several third-party software programs you can use to defragment your disk. In addition, if you are using DOS 6, you can use the DEFRAG command, discussed next, to correct fragmented files. If you are not using DOS 6 or later, you should upgrade your system to the latest DOS version now.

BEFORE YOU DEFRAGMENT YOUR DISK

When you defragment your disk, a software program might move each file's contents in order to place the information into consecutive sectors on your disk. Do not defragment your disk unless you have current backups of the files on your disk. Should an error occur when you are defragmenting a file, the file or worse yet, your disk's contents may be damaged or destroyed.

To defragment your files using the DEFRAG command you must be at the DOS prompt. If you are currently running Windows, use Exit Windows... option from the Program Manager's File menu to end your Windows session. Next, from the DOS prompt (C:\>), type **DEFRAG** and press ENTER:

```
C:\> DEFRAG   <ENTER>
```

The DEFRAG command will run, examining your disk's contents. Next, DEFRAG will display its recommendation dialog box, as shown in Figure 34.1.

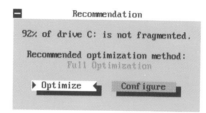

Figure 34.1 DEFRAG's Recommendation dialog box.

Select the Optimize option and press ENTER. DEFRAG will start defragmenting your disk, displaying a screen similar to the one shown in Figure 34.2.

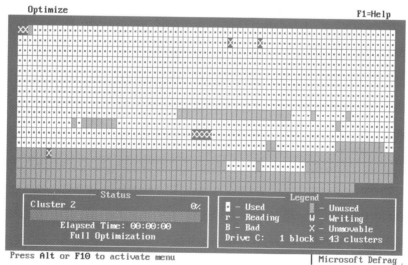

Figure 34.2 Defragmenting your disk.

Depending on your disk's size, the amount of time DEFRAG requires will differ. When DEFRAG completes, it will display a dialog box asking you if you want to defragment another drive or if you want to exit. Select the Exit option to return to DOS.

Note: If you are using disk compression software, such as DBLSPACE discussed in Lesson 32, DEFRAG will defragment both your compressed and uncompressed drives.

DEFRAGMENTING YOUR DISK DOES NOT RECOVER DISK SPACE

When you defragment files, you essentially move the files so that each file's contents reside in consecutive storage locations. By defragmenting files, you do not free up additional disk space. Instead, you simply make better use of the disk space that has already been consumed.

WHAT YOU NEED TO KNOW

Fragmentation of disk files is a natural consequence of disk use. If you notice that it takes a long time to run certain commands, they might be fragmented. In this lesson, you have learned how files get fragmented and how to repair them.

If you use Windows, there are several steps you can take to improve your system performance. In Lesson 35, you will learn how to fine-tune Windows memory use and how to speed up disk I/O operations within Windows. Before you continue with Lesson 35, however, make sure that you have learned the following key concepts:

- ✓ A fragmented file is a file whose contents are dispersed across your disk. A nonfragmented file, on the other hand, is stored in consecutive disk locations.

- ✓ Fragmented files decrease your system performance because it takes longer for the slow (mechanical) disk drive to access them.

- ✓ Files become fragmented naturally, when you create, edit, and delete files.

- ✓ Using software such as the DOS DEFRAG command, you can defragment your files and improve your system performance.

Lesson 35

Fine-Tuning Windows' Memory Use

In Lesson 13, you learned how to add memory to your PC. You have read that, when you add memory to your PC, you normally improve Windows performance instantly. Here's why. For Windows to run a program, the program must reside within the computer's memory. If Windows is running multiple programs, each program must reside in memory. The more memory your PC holds, the more programs Windows can load into memory at one time.

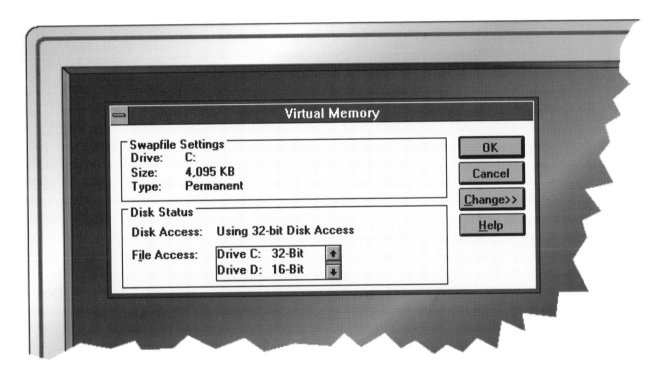

If you don't have unlimited memory, however, Windows periodically moves one program out of memory to disk to make room for other programs. If you are using Windows on a 386-based computer or higher (486 or Pentium), you can improve your system performance by increasing the amount of disk space Windows can use to swap programs in this way. In addition, several lessons in this book have discussed ways you can improve your computer's disk performance. As you will learn in this lesson, depending on your disk controller type, you may be able to improve Windows performance quickly by letting Windows itself (not the BIOS), control disk operations. This lesson examines ways you can "fine-tune" Windows performance. By the time you finish this lesson, you will understand the following key concepts:

- How Windows uses virtual memory

- How to display and set Windows virtual memory use

- How to improve Windows performance by speeding up disk operations

UNDERSTANDING AND USING VIRTUAL MEMORY

In Lesson 13, you examined your PC's random access memory (RAM). Today, most PCs sold have at least 2Mb of RAM. Those users who want the best performance within Windows should use 4 to 8Mb (or more) of RAM. The RAM that resides in your computer is *physical memory*, you can see it, touch it, and when programs run, they are stored in it.

Virtual Memory

As you know, Windows lets you run multiple programs at the same time. Depending on the number of programs you run, Windows and the programs can quickly use up your computer's physical memory. Thus, Windows uses a technique called *virtual memory* to trick the programs into thinking your computer has more memory than the physical RAM. Virtual memory combines your computer's RAM chips with a large *swap file* on your disk.

For a program to run, the program must reside in your computer's physical memory. When you run multiple programs at the same time, Windows moves inactive programs from physical memory to the swap file on disk. Should you select the program's window for use, Windows will move the program back into memory, possibly swapping a different program out to the swap file. Because your programs think your computer has more memory than is actually present, the nonexistent memory is called *virtual* memory. The amount of virtual memory available to Windows controls the number of programs you can run at one time.

Windows can use a permanent or temporary swap file. If you use a permanent swap file, a large part of your disk will be consumed to hold the file. However, the permanent swap file significantly improves Windows performance. If you use a temporary swap file, you can reduce the amount of hard disk space Windows consumes, but your performance can suffer. Most users should use a permanent swap file. To change your swap file settings, select the 386 Enhanced icon from the Control Panel. Windows will display the 386 Enhanced dialog box, shown in Figure 35.1.

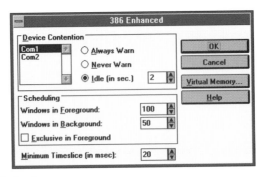

Figure 35.1 The 386 Enhanced dialog box.

Select the Virtual Memory button. Windows will display the Virtual Memory dialog box shown in Figure 35.2. Note the Type field to determine if you are using a permanent or temporary swap file:

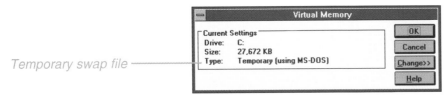

Figure 35.2 *The Virtual Memory dialog box.*

If you are already using a permanent swap file, select the Cancel option to close the dialog box. If you are using a temporary swap file, you can improve your system performance by clicking on the Change button to select a permanent swap file. Windows will expand the Virtual Memory dialog box, as shown in Figure 35.3. Within the dialog box, note the New Settings field:

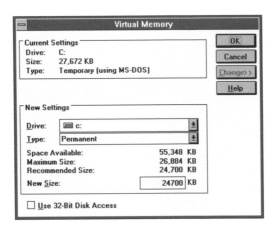

Figure 35.3 *The expanded Virtual Memory dialog box.*

The field lets you select which disk you want Windows to create the permanent swap file on, as well as the swap file size. Normally, Windows specifies a swap file size that is much larger than you require. You might want to specify a swap file size that is 2/3 of the size shown. To specify a new swap file size, click on the New Size field using your mouse and type in the desired size. Next, select the OK option. Windows will display a dialog box asking you to verify your changes. Select Yes. Next, Windows will display a dialog box asking you if you want to restart your computer. Select the Restart Now option. When Windows restarts, it will use your new permanent swap file.

SPEEDING UP DISK OPERATIONS

Because Windows lets you run multiple programs at the same time, Windows must protect one program from another. If two programs print at the same time, Windows must intercept the printouts to ensure that the program that asked for the printer first prints first, and two printouts are not garbled. To help Windows protect one program from another, Windows uses a special capability of the PC called *protected mode*. When programs run in protected mode, they cannot directly access a device or the computer memory in use by a second program. Unfortunately, DOS and your computer's BIOS chip, which oversees disk input and output operations, run in the computer's *real mode*.

Normally, to perform a disk read or write operation, Windows changes from protected mode to real mode and then asks the BIOS chip to perform the operation. When the operation completes, Windows changes back to protected mode. Unfortunately, the constant switching between protected and real mode is very time consuming and slows down your system performance. Fortunately, most disk drives support 32-bit protected mode operations. When you use these operations, you let Windows perform the disk input and output operations normally performed in real mode by the BIOS. In this way, your system performance increases tremendously.

To select 32-bit disk operations, select the Control Panel and double-click your mouse on the 386 Enhanced icon. Windows will display the 386 Enhanced dialog box, previously shown in Figure 35.1. Click your mouse on the Virtual Memory button. Windows will display the Virtual Memory dialog box, previously shown in Figure 35.2. Note the Type field to determine how Windows is accessing your disk:

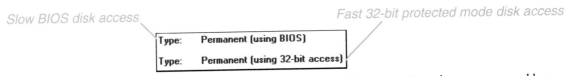

If you are currently using 32-bit disk access operations, close the dialog box. If you are using a battery-powered laptop computer, check with your computer manufacturer to determine if your computer supports 32-bit disk access before continuing.

If your system is currently using BIOS disk access, click your mouse on the Change button. Windows will expand the Virtual Memory dialog box as previously shown in Figure 35.3. Note the small check box that appears at the bottom of the dialog box:

Click your mouse on the check box, placing an X in the box to enable 32-bit disk access. Next, select the OK option. Windows will display a dialog box asking you to verify your changes. Select Yes. Next, Windows will display the Warning dialog box shown in Figure 35.4 that states 32-bit disk access may be unreliable on some battery powered computers.

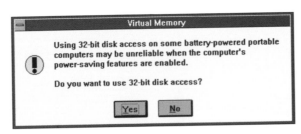

Figure 35.4 Windows 32-bit disk warning dialog box.

If you are not using a battery-powered laptop computer or if you have verified with your computer manufacturer that 32-bit disk access is supported, select Yes. Windows will then display the dialog box shown in Figure 35.5, asking you if you want restart your computer now or to continue working.

Figure 35.5 *Windows prompt to restart your computer.*

Select the Restart Now option to restart Windows and put your changes into use. When Windows restarts, it will use the faster 32-bit protected mode disk access.

Note: *Should Windows fail to start after you select 32-bit disk access, your disk controller does not support 32-bit operations. In such cases, edit the file SYSTEM.INI, which resides in the WINDOWS directory using an editor such as EDIT, provided with DOS. Within the file, locate the 32BitDiskAccess entry and change it to Off, as shown here:*

```
32BitDiskAccess=Off
```

Save your file change to disk and restart Windows.

WHAT YOU NEED TO KNOW

When you use many programs in Windows, you can use up all of your RAM. You have learned in this lesson how Windows deals with requests for more memory and how you can fine-tune Windows for your memory requirements.

In Lesson 36, you will learn how to use the MSD command, provided with DOS and Windows, to display key information about your system. As you will learn, MSD is very valuable troubleshooting tool. Before you continue with Lesson 36, make sure that you have learned the following key concepts:

✓ Windows uses virtual memory to give programs the illusion that they have more memory than is physically installed in their system. Virtual memory combines your computer's RAM with a swap file on disk. Windows moves inactive programs to the swap file to free up memory for the active programs.

✓ You can improve Windows performance (at the cost of disk space) by selecting a permanent swap file. To select a permanent swap file, use the Control Panel 386 Enhanced icon.

✓ Windows lets you improve the speed of disk read and write operations by selecting 32-bit disk access. To select 32-bit disk access, use the Control Panel 386 Enhanced icon.

Lesson 36

Troubleshooting with MSD

MSD is a utility program provided with DOS and Windows that you can use to examine your system configuration. MSD is an acronym for Microsoft Diagnostic. Using MSD, you can display information about your computer's memory use, port and IRQ settings, and much more. This lesson examines the MSD command in detail. By the time you finish this lesson, you will understand the following key concepts:

- How to use MSD to display key system settings

- How to print an MSD report ideal for use with technical support personnel

- How to browse through the PC's current memory use

MSD is a very powerful program. Using MSD you can detect and avoid possible hardware conflicts, which reduces future troubleshooting nightmares.

STARTING MSD

MSD is a utility program that you run from the DOS prompt. Do not run MSD with Windows active—you won't get correct results. Instead, exit Windows and start MSD from the DOS prompt, as shown here:

```
C:\> MSD    <ENTER>
```

MSD will start, displaying its main menu, as shown in Figure 36.1. From MSD's main menu you can determine specifics about your hardware, as discussed next.

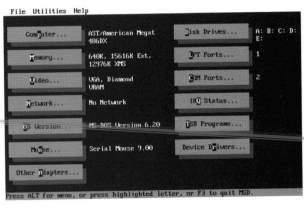

Figure 36.1 *MSD's main menu.*

DISPLAYING COMPUTER SPECIFICS

The MSD Computer option lets you display information about your processor, BIOS, and bus types. To display this information, press **P** at the MSD main menu. MSD will display the Computer dialog box, as shown in Figure 36.2. To return to the MSD main menu, press ENTER.

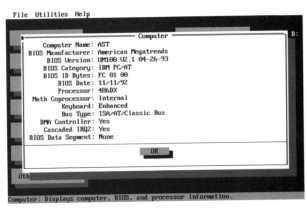

Figure 36.2 *The MSD Computer dialog box.*

Note: *You don't need to memorize the shortcut key for each option—they are visibly highlighted on the screen.*

DISPLAYING MEMORY SPECIFICS

The MSD Memory option lets you display information about your system memory use, such as the amount of conventional and extended memory, as well as your current use of the upper-memory area. To display this memory information, press **M** at the MSD main menu. MSD will display the Memory dialog box, as shown in Figure 36.3.

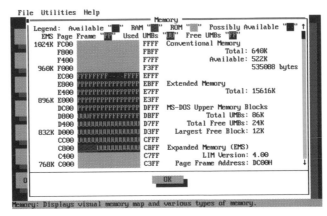

Figure 36.3 *The MSD Memory dialog box.*

If you press your keyboard's UP ARROW and DOWN ARROW keys, you can scroll through additional information. Use the legend that appears at the top of your screen to understand your memory use.

DISPLAYING VIDEO SPECIFICS

The MSD Video option lets you display specifics about your system's video capabilities, such as the display type, presence of a local bus, and the current video mode. To display the video specifics, press **V** at the MSD main menu. MSD will display the Video display dialog box, as shown in Figure 36.4.

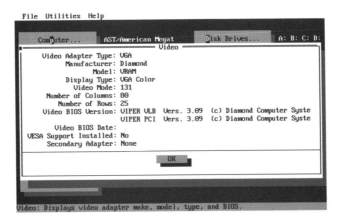

Figure 36.4 *The MSD Video dialog box.*

Video cards support several different text and graphics modes. Different text modes normally control the number of colors that can be used and the number of character rows and columns. Normally, the PC displays 25 rows with no more than 80 characters on each row.

When you work from the DOS prompt, you can normally ignore the video mode. Windows users, on the other hand, might want to experiment with different video modes (as discussed in Lesson 20) to determine the number of colors and resolution that best meets their needs. To return to the MSD main menu, press ENTER.

DISPLAYING NETWORK SPECIFICS

DISPLAYING NETWORK SPECIFICS

The MSD Network option lets you display specifics about your system's network, such as the network name, network BIOS, and so on. To display the network specifics, press **N** at MSD's main menu. MSD will display the Network dialog box, as shown in Figure 36.5. To return to the MSD main menu, press ENTER.

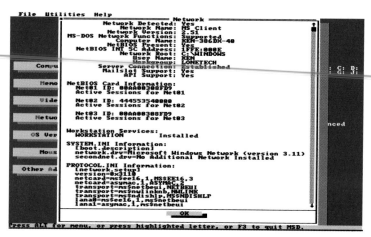

Figure 36.5 *The MSD Network dialog box.*

DISPLAYING OPERATING SYSTEM SPECIFICS

The MSD Operating System option lets you display specifics about the current operating system, such as current version number, boot disk, and DOS location (conventional or high memory area). To display the operating system specifics, press **O** at the MSD main menu. MSD, in turn, will display the OS Version dialog box, as shown in Figure 36.6. To return to the MSD main menu, press ENTER.

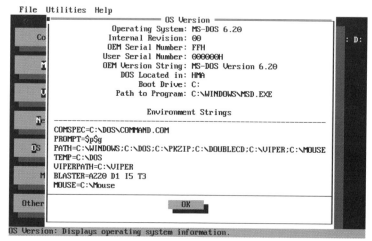

Figure 36.6 *The MSD OS Version dialog box.*

DISPLAYING MOUSE SPECIFICS

The MSD Mouse option lets you display specifics about your mouse, such as the mouse driver type and version, the mouse IRQ, and mouse sensitivity. To display the mouse settings, press U at MSD's main menu. MSD will display the Mouse dialog box, as shown in Figure 36.7. To return to the MSD main menu, press ENTER.

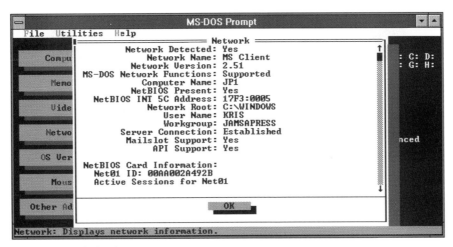

Figure 36.7 The MSD Mouse dialog box.

DISPLAYING ADAPTER SPECIFICS

The MSD Other Adapters option lets you display specifics about other hardware adapters, such as a joystick. To display adapter specifics, press A at the MSD main menu. MSD will display the Other Adapters dialog box, as shown in Figure 36.8. To return to MSD's main menu, press ENTER.

Figure 36.8 The MSD Other Adapters dialog box.

233

The MSD Disk Drives option lets you display specifics about your disk drives, such as the type, size, available space, and layout. To display the disk drive specifics, press **D** at MSD's main menu. MSD will display the Disk Drive dialog box, as shown in Figure 36.9.

If the disk drive settings shown are not correct, you will very likely need to update your computer's CMOS settings, as discussed in Lesson 6. To return to the MSD main menu, press ENTER.

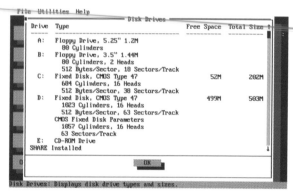

Figure 36.9 *The MSD Disk Drive dialog box.*

DISPLAYING LPT PRINTER PORT SPECIFICS

The MSD LPT Ports option lets you display specifics about your LPT printer ports, such as the port address and whether or not the computer sees a printer attached to the port. To display printer port specifics, press L at the MSD main menu. MSD will display the LPT Ports dialog box, as shown in Figure 36.10.

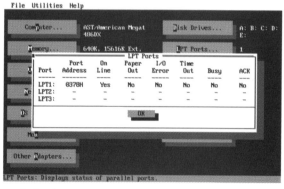

Figure 36.10 The MSD LPT Ports dialog box.

If you are having trouble with a printer, use MSD to make sure the computer sees the printer. To return to the MSD main menu, press Enter.

DISPLAYING SERIAL PORT SETTINGS

The MSD COM Ports option lets you display specifics about your system's serial ports, such as their current port address and data communication settings. To display the serial port settings, type C at the MSD main menu. MSD, in turn, will display the COM ports dialog box as shown in Figure 36.11.

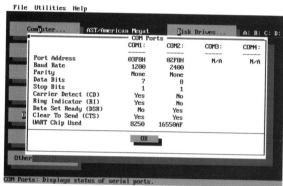

Figure 36.11 The COM Ports dialog box.

If you experience conflicts between serial port devices, such as a modem and mouse, use the COM Ports dialog box to verify that two devices are not using the same port address. Likewise, if you have trouble printing to a printer connected to a serial port, use this dialog box to examine the current port settings. The documentation that accompanied your printer will specify the settings the port must match. To return to the MSD main menu, press ENTER.

DISPLAYING IRQ SPECIFICS

As you read in Lesson 8, IRQ is an acronym for interrupt request. As you install different hardware cards, you need to be aware of each card's interrupt request line. Each card uses a unique IRQ line to signal the processor (to interrupt the processor) to request processing. For example, each time you move the mouse, the mouse interrupts the processor to tell it about the move. To display your PC's current IRQ settings, press **Q** at the MSD main menu. MSD will display the IRQ Settings dialog box, as shown in Figure 36.12.

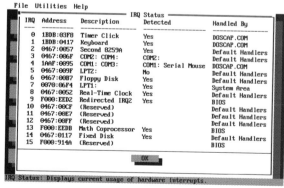

Figure 36.12 The MSD IRQ Settings dialog box.

If you are using an older PC based on an 8-bit bus (see Lesson 4), your system will support 8 IRQ lines, numbered 0 through 7. Table 36.2 lists the devices that normally correspond to these IRQ lines.

IRQ Number	Device
0	Timer
1	Keyboard
2	Available
3	COM2
4	COM1
5	Hard disk controller
6	Floppy disk controller
7	LPT1

Table 36.2 Devices that normally correspond to IRQ 0 through 7 on an 8-bit bus.

If you are using a 286-based PC or higher, your system will use 16 IRQ lines, numbered 0 through 15. Table 36.3 lists the devices normally assigned to these IRQ lines.

IRQ Number	Device	IRQ Number	Device
0	Timer	8	Real time clock
1	Keyboard	9	Redirected as IRQ2
2	Cascaded	10	Available
3	COM2	11	Available
4	COM1	12	Available
5	LPT2	13	Math coprocessor
6	Floppy disk controller	14	Hard disk controller
7	LPT1	15	Available

Table 36.3 Devices normally associated with IRQ 0 though 15.

To support the 16 IRQ levels, your PC uses two special chips called *interrupt controllers*. The first controller chip corresponds to interrupts 0 through 7 and the second to interrupts 8 through 15. To access this second set of interrupts, your PC actually steals the line for IRQ 2 and uses it for a special purpose. To activate one of the interrupts on the second controller, the PC sends a signal on IRQ 2. In this way, IRQ 2 is said to be "cascaded." When a signal is sent on IRQ 2, the second interrupt controller jumps into action. Thus, your PC really only supports 15 interrupt request lines.

If you examine different hardware cards, such as a modem or a mouse, for example, you might find that the card's default setting is IRQ 2. As you just learned, however, IRQ 2 is not really used. When you set a card to IRQ 2, the signal is transparently routed to IRQ 9. If you examine the previous MSD IRQ Status dialog box, things should make more sense. As you can see, MSD lists 16 IRQs. IRQ 2 is set to something called Second 8259A—that's the second interrupt controller. If you examine IRQ 9, you will see that it corresponds to the Redirected IRQ 2.

When you need to assign an IRQ to a new device, search the MSD screen for a (Reserved) entry. These entries are available for use.

QUICKLY LOCATING AVAILABLE IRQs

When you install a new hardware card, you might need to assign an IRQ (interrupt request) line to the card. Each card in your system must have a unique IRQ. To determine an available IRQ, perform these steps:

1. Invoke the MSD command from the DOS prompt.

2. Press **Q** to select the IRQ Settings option.

3. From the list of IRQs, search for a (Reserved) entry. These entries are available for use.

DISPLAYING INFORMATION ON MEMORY-RESIDENT PROGRAMS

A memory-resident program is a program that remains active in your computer's memory until you restart your system. Many device drivers, for example, are implemented as memory resident programs. Memory-resident programs are sometimes called *TSR* or terminate-and-stay-resident (in-memory) programs. The MSD TSR Programs option lets you display specifics about memory-resident programs. To display specifics on memory-resident programs, press **T** at the MSD main menu. MSD will display the TSR Programs dialog box, as shown in Figure 36.13.

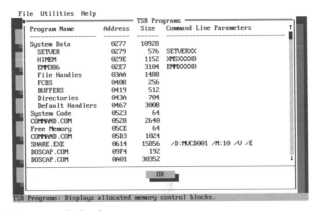

Figure 36.13 The MSD TSR Programs dialog box.

If you press your keyboard's UP ARROW and DOWN ARROW keys, you can scroll through the list of memory-resident programs. To return to the MSD main menu, press ENTER.

DISPLAYING DEVICE DRIVER SPECIFICS

A device driver is special software that lets your computer use a hardware device. Lesson 28 examines device drivers in detail. The MSD Device Drivers option lets you display device driver specifics such as the corresponding filename, the number of the devices the driver controls, the segment and offset address of the driver's header, and device attributes. To display device driver specifics, press **R** at MSD's main menu. MSD will display the Device Driver dialog box, as shown in Figure 36.14.

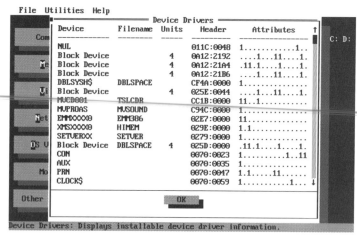

Figure 36.14 The MSD Device Drivers dialog box.

If a device driver does not specify a filename, the device driver is built into DOS. The filenames listed correspond to the device driver files that were installed from your CONFIG.SYS file when your system booted. The attributes specify different device characteristics.

Table 36.4 lists the meanings of the different device attributes. To return to the MSD main menu, press ENTER. For more specifics on device attributes, refer to the book *DOS Programming: The Complete Reference*, Osborne/McGraw-Hill, 1991.

Attribute Bit	Meaning If Set
0	This character device corresponds to the standard input device
1	This character device corresponds to the standard output device
2	This character device is the NUL device
3	This device is the CLOCK$ device
4	This character device supports fast I/O operations through Int 29H
6	This block device supports logical drive mapping and generic functions
7	This device supports IOCTL services
11	This device supports driver functions 0DH, 0EH, and 0FH
13	This device supports driver functions 10H and 02H
15	This device is a character device

Table 36.4 Meaning of device driver files.

PRINTING MSD REPORTS

Before you call a company's technical support, you need first to do some of your own homework. One of the best places to start is to print a copy of your MSD settings. To do so, press the ALT-F keyboard combination to select MSD's File menu, shown in Figure 36.15. Select the Print option.

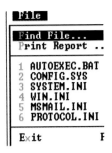

Figure 36.15 The MSD File menu.

If the company's technical support asks you for specific system settings, you will very likely find the settings within your MSD reports. In fact, you might even want to fax the reports to the technical support person.

GETTING MORE FROM MSD

If you are an experienced user, take time to examine the tools provided on MSD's Utilities menu. Using these tools, you can examine your system's memory use in detail, test the printer connections, and change various CONFIG.SYS and AUTOEXEC.BAT settings.

EXITING MSD

To exit the MSD program back to DOS, press the **F3** function key or press the ALT-F keyboard combination to select the File menu. From the File menu, choose Exit.

WHAT YOU NEED TO KNOW

Congratulations! By completing the lessons presented throughout this book, you are well on your way to fast PC performance, easy software upgrades, and elimination of many costly hardware repair bills. Before you continue on your way, however, make sure that you have learned the following key concepts:

✓ The MSD command provided with DOS and Windows can provide you with specifics about your computer's current hardware use.

✓ Using MSD, for example, you can determine which interrupt request (IRQ) lines are currently in use and avoid having to troubleshoot time-consuming IRQ conflicts.

✓ Before you call a company's technical support, you should print a copy of MSD's current settings. In many cases, you might want to fax the printout to the technical support personnel.

Index

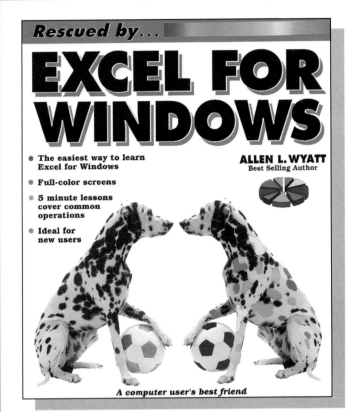

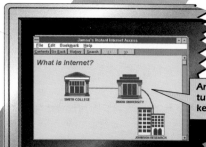